Praise for *Teacher Misery*

"Wow! Get ready to learn more than *Urban Dictionary* could ever possibly teach you. The chapter on Furries is one of the most original and hilarious things I've ever read! I dare you not to laugh out loud!"

–Robin O'Bryant, *New York Times* bestselling author of
Ketchup is a Vegetable and Other Lies Moms Tell Themselves

"If you are brave enough to be outraged by one horror story after another, then read this book for a compelling perspective on the challenges facing American teachers nowadays. In one page-turning short-chapter after another --- each twisted, hilarious, sad, and scary --- Jane Morris gives us a beautifully written exposé about the worst sides of today's students, parents and school administrators. The book is tragic, entertaining, and completely jaded."

–Bruce Tulgan, bestselling author of
Not Everyone Gets a Trophy: How to Manage the Millenials

"I shook my head. I winced. I shuddered. I laughed out loud. In my book, those are the four qualities of a masterpiece. Jane Morris not only lifts the curtain on the horror teachers in our country face every day, but shows that her chosen profession is every bit as dangerous as a waitress at Waffle House."

–Laurie Notaro, *New York Times* bestselling author of
The Idiot Girls' Action-Adventure Club

"Jane Morris, author of *Teacher Misery*, either has the patience of a saint or is certifiably insane, I can't decide which. Eh, who cares, because the stories she tells are unbelievable and yet, I'm positive they're true. This book left me laughing and reaching for a stiff drink – it's only a few more years until my kids grow up and become dumb ass teenagers."

–Jen Mann, *New York Times* bestselling author of
People I Want to Punch in the Throat

"As the daughter of two teachers, I've heard a lot about misbehaving students, parents, and administrators in my time, but none of it compared to the stories in *Teacher Misery*. Funny, freakish, and full of moments that make me glad I didn't follow in my parents' footsteps!"

–Sarah Knight, bestselling author of
*The Life-Changing Magic of Not Giving a F*ck*

"As a parent, I've seen the ridiculousness of the "my-super-special-snowflake" mentality playing out in preschools and elementary schools (so far), and I have always hoped that teachers privately called out nutty parents and resulting a-hole kids. I'm so glad that they do! At least this author does. And the resulting book where she dishes on the truth about trying to teach in this culture is hilarious informative, and insightful. But it will probably have you looking into private school so start saving."

–Stefanie Wilder Taylor, *New York Times* bestselling author of
–Sippy Cups Are Not for Chardonnay

"A compelling answer to anyone thoughtless enough to assert that teachers have it easy. This book shows that teaching is a tough, often maligned profession… yet brave and compassionate teachers keep coming back."

–John Owens, author of
Confessions of a Bad Teacher

"As with any good comedy, there is truth hidden within its pages. As funny as it is shocking."

–Librarything

"Morris isn't afraid to tackle the tough issues: drugs, schoolyard violence, and furries in the classroom, just for starters. I believe every word she wrote, and mourn our species just a little bit. You don't need to work with or have children to enjoy the book--if you've ever met a child, you'll see madness you recognize."

–Clint Looney, author of
*Ward of the Flies: A Child Counselor's F*ck-My-Life True Story*

"Eye-opening, intriguing and insightful."

–Night Reads

"Compelling."

–Goodreads

"I LOVE THIS BOOK. *Teacher Misery* perfectly encapsulates the comical misery that has become the teaching profession. As a teacher myself, while reading through these hilariously absurd anecdotes, I laughed hysterically, cried sympathetically, and by the end just straight up put my head in my hands, assuming the same "I-give-up" position that often gets me through a day in the classroom. If you're a teacher, this book will not inspire you to fall back in love with your profession, but it will make you thank the sweet heavens that SOMEONE out there understands. An important read for teachers and non-teachers alike-- *Teacher Misery* paints an amusing and thoroughly entertaining picture of what has become of our education system, without detracting from the overall point that what teachers have to put up with today is complete, utter, unacceptable insanity."

–Emily Lerman, author of Emily'sPosts.com

"Equal parts funny, shocking and a bit terrifying! When I remembered these stories are real, I couldn't help but laugh and cry at the same time at the state that our school system appears to be in and how farcical it all seems to be. This book speaks to the experiences of teachers and other public service workers alike. Hopefully it will help begin the reflection process and provide the impetus for us to take action toward the much needed change our school system needs and our children deserve."

–Michael Mantell, MSW, New York, New York

'Teacher Misery hit so close to home for me it's as if Ms. Morris and I work in the same school! This book truly shows the hilarity and sometimes downright ridiculousness of the teaching profession. I was laughing throughout the whole book! If you are a teacher or know a teacher, this book is definitely for you!"

–Erinn Keane, 3rd grade teacher, New York, New York

"Laughed until I cried, couldn't put it down. Every teacher should read this book! And to think I got suspended in 12th grade for saying the "f" word, ten short years ago. My how times have changed. I'm glad someone finally had the guts to tell it how it really is!"

–Amanda Marfeo, 5th grade teacher, Hopewell Junction, New York

"I love everything about this book. So funny and so true! I could seriously read these stories over and over again."

–Jackie Creasey, 8th grade math teacher, Anne Arundel, Maryland

"If you're going into this book with the notion that teaching is boring, you will be pleasantly (or unpleasantly, depending on your mindset) surprised. If there's one thing that can be said about being a teacher, it makes for great stories to share while drinking bottomless margaritas at the end of the week. This book is like that, but without the hangover."

–Alexis Lambusta, 6th-8th Special Education teacher, Virginia

"Every day for the past ten years, I have primarily worked in the most difficult inner-city schools. While most of my friends thoroughly enjoy the outlandish and almost unbelievable stories I've had to tell, they don't actually LIVE the horror like I do. I cannot express the sheer joy I experienced when I stumbled upon Teacher Misery on Instagram! Finally, someone who fully understood my plight and represented it in compact and hysterical posts. I immediately felt a connection as a fellow educator and as someone who has a complete love/hate relationship with her job. Obsessive? Perhaps, but I just can't get enough of *Teacher Misery*."

–Laura Cipolletti, 6th-8th grade English teacher, Cleveland, Ohio

"This stuff cannot be made up! I laughed until I cried, cheered her on, and got red with fury at some of her encounters with parents and administration. *Teacher Misery* shows that teachers really are superheroes, because no matter how many times we get knocked down, we come right back the next day to try again."

-Lauren Cocroft, 6th grade math teacher, Memphis, Tennessee

Teacher
Misery

JANE MORRIS

Truth Be Told Publishing

Cover design by Stacey Hill Designs
Author drawing by NatalieDee.com

ISBN: 978-0692697955
ISBN-13: 0692697950

FOR M,

Always for you

CONTENTS

Part III. Administration

Afterward

"School is indeed training for later in life because it teaches absurdity."

Jules Henry

PREFACE

While there is a pervasive myth that being a teacher in America is a relatively easy job (good hours, holidays and summers off, tenure etc.), many know otherwise. Many are aware of the shocking statistic that close to fifty percent of teachers quit within their first five years. Twenty percent of all teachers quit every year after that. If you had to guess why there is such a significant turnover rate just picture a new teacher, full of optimism, creativity and heart, whose only available placement is in a "rough" urban school, teaching six classes a day, with up to 40 students per class. You might imagine the incredible workload of grading hundreds of papers per week, the after school activities for no extra pay and the extremely low, stagnant wages. But these conditions don't come as a surprise to new teachers. They've observed and interned in classrooms and were probably quite aware of these circumstances before entering the classroom themselves. They know what they're getting into, and they still do it.

So why do half of them quit? It's not the low salary or the enormous workload- it's the absurdity: the absurdity of a parent who blames their son's act of arson on a teacher (for causing him low self-esteem); a student who doesn't get so much as a slap on the wrist for selling drugs in class; and an administrator whose best advice is to "treat kids like sacks of shit." It's the foolishness of a parent cursing out a teacher on the phone and the teacher getting in trouble for hanging up. It's the senselessness of a policy which states that a teacher should not call 911 in a medical emergency, for it is not her call to make. It's the craziness of a parent who claims that although her son never came to class, he should be given a passing grade because he has knowledge in his brain but cannot demonstrate that knowledge in written or verbal form. It is the meaninglessness of official observations done by administrators that list "not writing in a straight

1

line" and "blinds not pulled up evenly" as areas for improvement. And it is especially the general disregard for teachers that allows them to be publicly bullied and harassed on rating websites. Combine these absurd circumstances with the low wages and high workload and it's a recipe for teacher misery.

In 1969, Bel Kaufman published a novel entitled *Up the Down Staircase* based on her real life experiences as a teacher of English in an inner city high school. It has been translated into sixteen languages, made into an award-winning film, and staged as a play numerous times. Its title has even become a much-repeated phrase in America.

As an English teacher in the year 2016, reading *Up the Down Staircase* is like a hilarious romp through a field of small potatoes. Isn't it ironic that going up a staircase specifically labeled for going downstairs was a problem in 1969, whereas students having sex completely naked on the staircase is barely even a punishable offense in 2015? But perhaps what is more hilarious (and horrifying) is the parent of one of those students who argues that it is the school's fault for not including "no sex on the staircase" as an official school rule.

Think you know the modern teaching profession? I'd bet you my meager retirement savings that you don't.

NOTE

Everything in this book, with the exception of names and locations, is true. This is a compilation of my experiences during the first five years of my teaching career. All names have been changed, including my own, to protect identities. (There are a handful of experiences which I saw other teachers endure, and they were too good not to include.) But if any lawyers or other intimidating individuals ever ask, nothing in this book is true, it is fiction based on real life events.

Memento mori is a Latin phrase which means, "Remember you will die." It refers to a genre of art that spans throughout history and sought to remind people of their mortality, mainly through depicting an image of a human skull. It was like a more depressing version of carpe diem (or YOLO, if you're an idiot). During my first year of teaching, a fellow new teacher and I shared many of the same woes. One day, in response to a long email filled with my complaints and whining, she sent me the following response: "When this job feels overwhelming, remind yourself that one day you will die!" She also included a happy, smiling skull. She is no longer a teacher. She quit in her 5th year.

While this was meant to be a joke, it brings up a larger point. When faced with the trials and difficulties of everyday life, we must ask ourselves if it is worth it on a grander scale. The answers we find can help determine if we are doing what we are supposed to do. I keep a replica of a skull on my desk to remind me that in the grand scheme, none of the bullshit matters, and yes, it is worth it. But here I will use it as an ellipsis, and as a humorous reminder that when the job just seems too hard, there are always two things to look forward to- retirement and death.

INTRODUCTION

I have the unique opportunity of teaching in an American high school that integrates many races, religions, and economic backgrounds. A public school usually represents the demographics of the community in which it resides. My school is situated right outside of a major American city. Students are enrolled from the poorest areas in the city, and the middle-class neighborhood surrounding the school. We also have several programs for gifted students, and many are bused in from the wealthiest areas in the county. The school is a demographical dream with almost a perfect mix of 25% Black, 25% Latino/Hispanic, 25% White and 25% Asian students. They derive from over 90 countries and speak more than 50 languages. It is a perfectly PC school for a study on our current educational system. I have students who barely speak English, students who can hardly read or write, and others who win National Merit scholarships to the best colleges in the country. I have students who go home to multi-million dollar mansions with indoor pools, and others who live in the back of a pickup truck with a tarp over it. There are students with parents who have medical, doctoral and law degrees and those with parents on welfare, in jail or in a homeless shelter.

Given the broad range of student backgrounds I have taught, I can honestly say that my unbelievably ridiculous and most challenging students don't fit a particular profile. There is no one demographic that is easier to teach than another. It is all equally difficult, just in different ways. And I should know. Before I started teaching at the school on which this book is based, I tried my hand at many teaching positions. I didn't discriminate. I needed money and health insurance, and there weren't many openings where I lived, so I took whatever was offered.

One of my most interesting experiences was at a psychiatric center. When I was hired, I was told that although this was a live-in facility for teens who had psychological problems, it would be like a regular teaching job. I would teach them about literature, and they would be well behaved since they were heavily medicated. I would even design my own curriculum and could order whatever books and supplies I wanted! This assignment seemed like every teacher's dream scenario: sedated students, an unlimited budget, and no curriculum restrictions!

Every day I ran from that place crying hysterically. I lasted two weeks. The security team told me that it was the longest any young female had ever stayed there. My classroom had bars on the windows, and no pens or pencils because the students could stab each other with them. They used big, thick markers instead. The students were mostly male, with one or two females. The classes probably should have been separated by gender, since one girl spent most of the class with another boy's hand down her pants (I was told to ignore them). They were all about 16 or 17 years old. I started out with some creative writing exercises. Instead of teaching anything, I spent almost all of the time in class telling them not to touch each other and running into the hallway screaming for help. I had to keep making the activities easier and easier because you cannot correct kids who have psychotic anger issues. Needless to say, they take it pretty personally.

The last time I corrected a student was during an activity that is usually reserved for elementary school kids. I had them write their names vertically on a piece of paper, and for each letter, they had to pick an adjective that described their personality in some way. We went around the room and shared. It went smoothly until one student shared his work. He had the letter t in his name, and he wrote "tree." I told him that he did an excellent job, but I had one question. How did the word tree describe him? He looked slowly from his paper to me, back and forth, three or four times, and then lunged at me from across the room. I was able to move out of the way and run into the hallway before he made any actual contact. The security guard in the hallway explained to me that this student had tried to murder a teacher when he was in public school. I couldn't believe it. She started going through the case histories of each student. Most were involved in extremely violent crimes.

"Haven't you read their case files?" she asked. "What case files?" I replied. "They didn't show you their files? Oh, I see. Come with me," she said. She led me to a huge conference room filled with big binders. Each binder was several inches thick and contained detailed histories about each student. Many were born addicted to heroin or crack. They were all severely mentally ill. One student suddenly popped into my head. "What about Roy? He doesn't seem to belong here. He is polite, calm and does all of his schoolwork."

"Roy!" she answered. "He's the worst one! He tried to kill his mother!"

"No way!" I exclaimed.

"Here look," she said as she slid his binder over to me. "He claimed that the devil told him to sleep with a knife under his pillow every night in case he had to stab his mother."

I opened Roy's binder. Holy shit. Indeed, he heard the voice of the devil telling him to kill his mother on a daily basis. He stabbed her in the arm once. Then he came up with a more diabolical plan. He put some silly putty on the ceiling in his bedroom and asked his mom if she could stand on a chair to help him remove it. She did, and he kicked the chair out from under her. She slammed down to the floor and severely broke her arm. As she cried out in agony on the floor, he looked down and called her a bitch.

I closed Roy's binder, thanked the nice security guard, and promptly left that facility, never to return. I never heard from them; not a phone call or even a paycheck. They were used to this.

That experience was extreme and not the average experience of a classroom teacher. However, at least these kids had valid excuses for their psychotic behavior- they were actually psychotic. In my "regular" teaching job, I encounter insane behavior on a daily basis, from students, their parents, and even school administrators.

All I ever wanted was to teach Shakespeare and Orwell, inspire kids to love reading and grade some essays. I didn't know I would be engaged in a daily psychological battle of wills. I had no idea that everything I said and did had to be extremely well thought out, to preempt any backlash from students and their parents.

It's not that all of the teaching experience is so horrible. It can be a lot of fun, and inspiring, and sometimes even downright rewarding. But the amount of bullshit far outweighs the good stuff. You just can't believe what it's like, and as you read through my experiences you probably won't. But I promise you, it is all real. And it isn't too out of the ordinary either.

I. STUDENTS

"One of the hardest things for kids to learn is that a teacher is human. One of the hardest things for a teacher to learn is not to try and tell them."

Alan Bennett

FURRIES

I have had the interesting experience of teaching "furry" students. For those of you who don't know what a furry is (I certainly didn't before I had them as students), allow me to explain. According to Wikipedia, "Furry Lifestylers" refers to a group of people who have "important emotional/spiritual connections with an animal or animals, real, fictional or symbolic." Being an animal lover myself, this seemed like something I could relate to. But this goes way beyond loving animals. Furries see themselves as "other than human" and "desire to become more like the furry species that they identify with." I mean, I really love dogs. Some might even say I'm obsessed with them. But I'm pretty sure I don't want to *be* one.

Furries take their furriness very seriously. They feel a deep kinship with a certain animal, and dress like that animal all the time, even at school. Many wear parts of the animal such as the ears and tail, or fake paws and an animal head. Each furry has a "fursona" or set of animal personality traits, which they use to role play in various forms, on the internet or at conventions, for example. These conventions, such as Anthrocon or ConFurence, draw thousands of people who share similar interests.

My first furry came to school on the first day wearing white ears and a long white tail pinned to the seat of his pants. It was so long that it dragged on the floor, picking up dust mites and other debris. I wasn't sure what his deal was, so

I didn't ask him about what he was wearing. He offered that information for the class soon after.

I paired the students up and asked them to interview each other as a typical first day of school activity. The poor girl who was partners with the furry had a hard time keeping a straight face during the interview. Next the students had to introduce their partners to the class. They merely had to share the names, nicknames and hobbies of their partner. When it was time for the furry and his partner to present, they both stood up. The girl turned bright red before she spoke. "This is Herbert. He likes to be called… umm… Zorra. He says he's a fox and-" Here Herbert interrupted with an irritated clarification. "I'm a *silver* fox." She held back a laugh and said, "He's a silver fox and is also… umm… He's pansexual? That's it." At that point, most of the class was laughing. Herbert was extremely annoyed. I tried to defuse the situation by asking a few clarifying questions.

"Herbert I think we are just a little confused. What do you mean when you say that you are a silver fox?" He took a deep breath and said, "I embody the spirit of a silver fox." The class was silent and waiting for my reaction. I calmly responded. "Okay, and what does it mean to be pansexual? I've never heard that word before." He was slightly less aggravated now that he saw I was merely curious and seeking knowledge. "Pansexual means that it's possible for me to be attracted to anyone."

I quickly realized that I had gotten myself into a sticky situation, and I should have just moved on to the next group. But I was genuinely curious. "So it's like someone who is bisexual?" I said, giving the class a serious look that meant they should not laugh. "No," he said. "I'm *pan*sexual. I don't subscribe to labels. I'm just attracted to whoever I'm attracted to, regardless of what gender or species they identify with." Another kid yelled out, "That means he's gay!" Before I could answer, another kid said, "No! That means he has sex with animals!"

"Okay, that's enough. Thank you for sharing Herbert and for being so open with the class. I appreciate it, and I learned something new today." Before he sat down he said, "Yeah I'd just like to say one thing. I'm sick of being called Cat Boy. I am *not* a cat; I am a *silver fox*! These are two very different animal spirits." Another kid yelled out, "Whatever Cat Boy!" and Herbert sat down with his arms crossed in anger.

The next day I met Herbert's furry girlfriend. Her name was Alice, but she insisted on being called Loculo, which is Latin for "coffin." She would not answer if you called her anything but Loculo. Loculo wore ears and a tail, but she also wore fake paw gloves. She refused to have anyone interview her, and she introduced herself to the class. She said that she was a wolf trapped inside a girl's body and that she identified with a gray wolf in almost every way. She also said that she is very selective about her "pack mates" and relates mostly to herbivores. No one questioned her or said a word, including me. Something told me that for this student, her "fursona" wasn't just a phase.

A few classes later I gave the students an assignment to create a fictional, future biography with an illustrated cover. This exercise was meant to be a way for them to picture what they might be successful at and well-known for later in life. I had them share their covers. Many students had silly, unrealistic drawings and ideas, but they had a lighthearted approach when sharing with the class. When Loculo shared her cover, the fear in the room was palpable. She stood up and showed the following drawing.

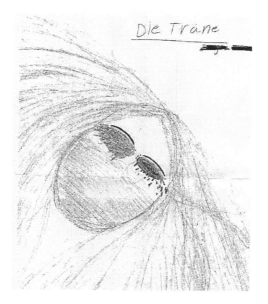

She said, "My biography is called die träne, which means 'the tear' in

German." That is all she said, as she stood there holding up this horrifying picture. I asked, "What is this picture of?" She said, "This is a victim of rape and murder." I looked around the room at the shocked faces. I tried to find some normalcy in this while maintaining composure. "And why did you choose to put this on the cover of your biography?" (Why was I asking more questions? This couldn't possibly lead to anywhere good.) She started to speak and stumbled over her words a few times. Finally she said, "I just find rapists and murderers interesting."

"Oh," I said. "So you are interested in psychology?"

"Yes," she answered.

Thank God, I thought.

"So you want to be a psychologist maybe? Perhaps work for the FBI as a profiler? Or a criminal psychologist?" I asked with hope.

"Yes," she responded quickly.

"Great!" I said. Then she looked at me as though she saw that I was trying to find some normality in what she was saying and said, "Actually no. *No.* I just like rapists and murderers."

I called Loculo's mom to discuss her daughter's behavior with her. She said, "Look, you're not telling me anything new. My daughter is in therapy almost every day of her life. This is nothing I don't know. But thanks for calling."

I had yet another furry encounter when I covered a class for another teacher. They had a creative writing assignment to complete with a partner. I couldn't help but notice two students were stroking each other like cats. They were also rubbing their noses on each other's cheeks very gently. When they began to lick each other, I got nervous. Another student saw my face and whispered, "They think they're cats. Just wait, they'll meow soon." It seemed like it had to be a joke but when I asked the teacher, he confirmed that they take their cat selves very seriously. He had arguments with the parents about whether or not their behavior was appropriate for the classroom. He gave up and just let them do their cat thing.

I would just like to add that it is perfectly okay for students to wear animal costumes in class, but hats are strictly forbidden.

THE ENTITLEMENT CHRONICLES

During my first week of teaching, it was suggested to me that I become an advisor for one of the school's clubs. When I did not immediately take on an advisory role for an organization of my choice, I was told that I was now the advisor to the school's newspaper. I thought it was weird that they couldn't find someone with more experience to run the paper, but I would soon find out why the position remained vacant.

The role of newspaper advisor had me babysitting sixty extremely self-righteous teenagers from three to midnight every other Friday night so they could finalize the paper. While the advisory role included a stipend, after all was said and done I was making about a dollar an hour. The worst part about my advisory role was that students received grades for their work on the paper, but the editors were the ones who assigned the grades, not me. I was tortured over grades that "technically" I assigned, when their classmates were the ones doing the actual grading. The editors often assigned grades for arbitrary reasons, and I would be left to defend those grades to the students and their parents.

For example, a few days after the first report card went out I received the following email:

To: Newspaper Advisor

From: Rolf's Parents

Subject: Grade

Dear Ms. Morris,

Why did you give our son Rolf a C in your journalism class? Clearly you cannot recognize the makings of a brilliant writer. When re-calculating Rolf's grade, we came to realize that most of the weight of his grade rested upon a single writing assignment. We read Rolf's article carefully and were impressed with what we saw. His work, which you gave a C, undoubtedly merited an A. We took it to a friend of ours who is a Global Distinguished Professor of Journalism at Some Fancy University and who formerly worked for a very prestigious newspaper. He agreed that Rolf's article merited an A.

With this in mind, we request that you complete a grade change form for Rolf as soon as possible to give him the grade that he unquestionably deserves.

Thank you for your attention in this matter,

Rolf's Parents

I read the article several times and did not feel it deserved an A. Perhaps the article would have earned a low B using a standard writing rubric, but definitely not an A. I asked various administrators for advice on how to handle this situation. After careful consideration, I decided to avoid the anguish of Rolf's parents complaining to the school board about my careless handling of the grading process in my class. After Rolf had apologized for his parents' email, I gave him the grade change they wanted. At least Rolf had manners.

But that was only the start of my newspaper miseries. A few weeks later I received the following email from an anonymous sender:

To: Newspaper Advisor

From: Anonymous Student

Subject: Thought you might want to know

Ms. Morris,

Just thought you'd want to know what your students think of you.

From,

A student on the newspaper staff

The following is a transcript of an instant message conversation that was cut and pasted into the email:

4U2NV: So what do you think of the new newspaper advisor?

DragonGrlZ: I think she's kind of dumb

4U2NV: I know! I can't stand her

DragonGrlZ: She never has anything useful to say about the paper

4U2NV: I feel like she's going to ruin the paper. We didn't work our asses off and win all those awards to have some idiot come and destroy it with her incompetence

DragonGrlZ: Yeah I hate seeing her sitting there rambling about random stuff

4U2NV: Do you even know where she came from or how she got this job?

DragonGrlZ: Who cares she's a moron

4U2NV: Seriously, we should talk to the principal

about getting someone more capable

DragonGrlZ: Perhaps we should talk to the staff when she's not there

4U2NV: I gotta go ttyl

Admittedly, I was unprepared to advise the newspaper. I had little journalism experience and almost no teaching experience. But I have advanced degrees from prestigious universities and can certainly teach about the writing process and properly edit an article. Looking back on it now, I should have deleted the email and pretended it never happened. But it hurt, and my boss had already seen my reaction and was on the case. Now I desperately wanted to know who had sent the email, and I wanted there to be consequences.

We had every computer expert in the building working on tracing the email. When they couldn't figure it out, we took it to the district's central office and then the school board. The person who sent the email was smart and left no tracks behind. So instead of punishing the kid who sent the email, the administration chose to focus on the kids who discussed my lack of competence in an online chat.

I had to attend a meeting with the two students, both sets of parents, the head of my department, and two assistant principals. We all got transcripts of the conversation. I had to endure the reading aloud of the conversation. After that the Ass. Principal asked the two students what they had to say for themselves. "4U2NV" said he was sorry, in a rather unapologetic way. "DragonGrlZ" launched into an angry diatribe about how she didn't feel she needed to apologize because she has a right to free speech. The head of my department said that she should be ashamed of the way she spoke about her teacher and that she should show more respect. The girl responded that she did nothing wrong. She didn't say these things to my face. It was a private conversation that was stolen, and she has a right to her opinion. Her father said, somewhat respectfully, that his daughter was right.

The girl said that there was nothing we could do to punish her. She was correct. Then she took the opportunity to start a discussion about my so-called incompetence. She said that the school should take this incident as an opportunity to investigate my performance and that there was truth in her opinion. I started to wonder if she was the one who sent me the anonymous email.

Interestingly, a few weeks later, another teacher had gotten into a huge argument with the same student over her arrogance. He pretty much tore her down in front of the class and made her cry. The next day his fiancé called him at school crying. She had received an email from him saying that he no longer loved her; he was cheating on her, and he wanted to break up. He did not send the email, but someone sent it, posing as him, from his school email account. When the school tried to trace where the email was sent from, it was the same IEP address of the email that I had received. But this still didn't prove anything. The teacher whose email was hacked quit at the end of the year.

I ended up having "DragonGrlZ" in my English class second semester. She almost never came to class and didn't make up much of the work. On the last day of class, she came up to me and said, "I want to talk to you about the C you are giving me in the class." I said what most teachers say. "I don't give out anything. You earn your grades, and you are never here and you never make up any work. You're lucky you even have a C." She looked at me with contempt and said, "Well, I feel that if a teacher isn't stimulating me enough in class then I have no reason to show up." I almost fell over. "I'm sorry you feel that way," I said, because I was a new teacher and didn't have the balls to tell her how I really felt. She spun around and walked out, and I almost kicked a desk across the room, but instead I did nothing because what could I have done?

PROCLAMATION OF INTENT TO STRANGLE

The staff members of the newspaper all receive a very long "proclamation" about what is expected of them and how they will be graded. They are supposed to sign the proclamation in acknowledgment of the grading policies and such. The fact that they all signed this document that explicitly stated what they would be graded on meant nothing to them. And since I was not the one who was essentially assigning the grades, at the end of the quarter, a lot of bullshit hit the fan. For example, I received the following email:

```
To: Newspaper Advisor

From: Hugh Jazzhole

Subject: My Grade

Ms. Morris,

    I just saw that I received a B for my production
grade. I know that I was late, and left early, but
it is not fair that I should lose a letter grade
because of that. By being late, I was not aware that
I was breaking a rule that would affect my grade. I
assumed my grade would be based on the QUALITY of my
work and not attendance. No other teacher would do
```

such a thing.

However, I understand that this is not a regular class. So I would not object to a few points being taken off. Yet according to my calculations, even if I get an A on all the other assignments, I would still receive a B for this grade because of the weighting. It is ridiculous for me to automatically receive a B because of attendance, especially because my tardiness made no difference to anyone. There are many things in this class that are unfair, yet I doubt that even real newspapers treat their employees so unfairly.

According to the official proclamation, one of the responsibilities of the advisor is to see that grades are given fairly. Simply put, I was not graded fairly. Therefore, it is your job to change my grade to something more reasonable. I expect this change to be made within the next week.

Hugh Jazzhole

I replied to Hugh with a clear outline of the parts of the proclamation that he signed (and the students *themselves* wrote). The lines stated that attendance is critical during production nights, and thus is a major part of their grade. While Hugh was busy stuffing his face at McDonalds, other students were working their asses off to make deadlines. I also said that as the advisor, I felt the grade was fair, and would not change it. I received the following email in return:

Ms. Morris,

I have read your statements but I'm afraid I remain unconvinced that I deserve the grade I received. I will briefly outline my reasoning below. However, if after reading my email you still feel that I deserve the grade I received then I will directly appeal my grade to the administration, and if necessary the district, in accordance with the student due process procedure outlined by the district and the state.

According to the highlighted sections of the proclamation, by being on the newspaper staff I agreed to:

a. adhere to all deadlines

b. accept the grades given to me by my student editors (although the advisor has the ability to override those grades)

In response to part A: As previously mentioned, my lateness did not affect my deadlines.

In response to part B: Accepting grades from peer editors does not mean I cannot request a change in grade if I was treated unfairly, and clearly this is the case. Regardless of what the class is and who is "teaching," students never have to accept a grade unconditionally. If students can protest a grade given in a regular class— taught by a professional teacher— then surely we can protest grades given by peers and overseen by an "advisor."

Additionally, I would like to point out the district's grading policy for grades 6-12, as stated in policy number 157 (refer to the link below). As mentioned in section A, "grades should ACCURATELY reflect a student's ACHIEVEMENT, and should be a FAIR representation of a student's PERFORMANCE." As I mentioned in my previous email, my grade was not the result of poor performance, but instead the result of breaking the rules (i.e. improper behavior). Grades are meant to measure academics and not behavior. If a student behaves poorly (like being late), teachers do not lower grades but seek proper disciplinary action instead.

You may think I am overreacting to this situation. However, it is a very big deal. First of all, because of the weighting, this grade may determine whether or not I receive an A for the quarter. As you know, quarter grades are factored into the GPA, and in this very competitive world, one B can make a big difference.

However, grades aside, this situation touches on much bigger issues such as fairness and respect. Any impartial observer would see that the grade I received was unfair. In addition, a person would need to be blind to see the lack of respect that I have received. My parents, teachers and administrators that I've interviewed can testify to how much of an asset I am to the newspaper and to this school. Yet I still get punished for the slightest offense. I consider this disrespectful.

Therefore, the main reason that I am treating this situation as such a big issue is that I see it as a blatant sign of disrespect. The least you can do for the work I have put into the paper is give me the grade I deserve. If such clear signs of unfairness are ignored, I will have to take further action in this matter. Please take my grievance seriously.

Hugh Jazzhole

I was outraged by the level of insolence Hugh showed in his language towards me. I had been stewing in the words of this email for an entire weekend, and come Monday morning I was fired up. I called Hugh into my classroom and told him that although he mentioned the fact that he felt disrespected, I could

23

not believe the level of disrespect he showed towards a teacher. As I said this, his lips started to shake. I thought of him putting my titles of teacher and advisor in quotes, took a deep breath and continued to rip into him. "How *dare* you speak to me that way? Do you really think that you will achieve your purpose, and get what you want, by treating me in such a way?" His lip was shaking violently, and he stuttered. "Well, do you?" I yelled. "Say something!"

Suddenly a wad of spit came from Hugh's mouth, and it rolled down his chin, mixing with a torrent of tears. He was so hysterical that he could not complete a sentence. "It's just that… I mean… It's not… I just…" I sat there and watched this little fit continue for several awkward minutes. He was embarrassing himself; snarfing, blubbering and exploding with phlegm. I really did feel sorry for him. He was a fucking mess.

Like an infant after a full blown tantrum, it took him a long bunch of crazy deep breaths and mini crying spells to calm himself. I asked him if he was under a lot of pressure to get straight A's. He nodded yes. He said that when his parents moved here from Korea they heard that Harvard was the best school. He was three years old at the time. Since then, they have been telling him that he must get into Harvard, or he will disgrace them. I told him that that is an awful lot of pressure and that if he wrote me a sincere apology letter, I would give him his stupid A. He did write me an apology letter, and while he was mostly full of shit, I had to see the sadness in his situation. A few months later when he received his rejection from Harvard, he sprawled out on the floor in the hallway of the school and refused to leave the building. His parents told him that if he didn't get accepted, he shouldn't come home. Hugh had enough problems, and I felt satisfied with my decision. Sometimes when teens try to act like arrogant adults it can be rather convincing (some are 6'3 with full beards, which doesn't help in this matter). But then they do something like cry uncontrollably over nothing, to remind you that they are just kids, and it can be very sobering. Poor Hugh.

My final newspaper odyssey that I'd like to share occurred on one of the late nights when I was in charge of fifty plus teens. Since I could only be in one room at once, and the students were in four or five different places, things could get quite chaotic. One Friday night at around 11 PM, after an already long week, a girl came into the room screaming that a kid was shooting a nail gun.

I later sent the following email:

To: Ass. Principal

From: Newspaper Advisor

Subject: Late Night Issue (nail gun)

Dear Ass. Principal,

We are having a major problem yet everyone has left the building for the night, including all the security guards. It is 11 o'clock on Friday night. I am here supervising the newspaper staff. Seymour Butts, the sports page editor, has been going into each of the classrooms and up and down the hallways shooting a makeshift nail gun. He is shooting very large nails (I have saved several of them) at the ceiling and other students. I asked him to leave, and he started a huge argument. He refused to leave. He yelled at the other students in the computer lab that it is bullshit that he should have to leave and that they should all vote on whether or not he should have to leave. I told him that we were not voting on anything, that he was acting recklessly, and that there was no discussion to be had. He announced, "This is fucking bullshit! Everyone should stand up to her! We don't have to take this shit! Fuck this!" Luckily, everyone ignored him, and he finally left the building.

If we could please meet about Seymour on Monday, I would appreciate it. Not only should he be off the paper, I'm sure you'll agree that there should be some disciplinary action taken.

Thanks,

J. Morris

The following week we met with Seymour and his father to discuss his behavior. Although I was there, I did not say anything, for there was no reason to. (Keep in mind that Seymour was in attendance at the meeting as well.) This is what occurred:

ASS. PRINCIPAL: Mr. Butts, as you know, we called you here today to discuss the incident that occurred at school last Friday night.

MR. BUTTS: I would hardly call it an incident.

ASS. PRINCIPAL: What your son did was very serious. He endangered many students, and while he may not have had malicious intent, he still acted very carelessly.

MR. BUTTS: I'll agree that what Seymour did was stupid, and I have discussed it with him. But do we need to have a meeting about it?

ASS. PRINCIPAL: Mr. Butts, I am glad that you discussed this matter with your son. But disciplinary action must be taken.

MR. BUTTS: Action *was* taken. He was grounded this weekend.

ASS. PRINCIPAL: Again, I am glad that you are taking this incident seriously, but the school must do something to send a message, not only to Seymour but to the rest of the students and community, that this dangerous behavior will not be tolerated.

MR. BUTTS: What are we talking about exactly?

ASS. PRINCIPAL: Well normally the police would be involved in an incident involving a weapon-

MR. BUTTS: Oh please! A weapon? A nail gun is not a weapon! Besides, he didn't bring the nail gun in to hurt people with it. He brought it to school to work on a project.

ASS. PRINCIPAL: That may be the case, but he still put many students in danger by using it in a reckless manner.

MR. BUTTS: Listen, Seymour is a seventeen-year-old boy, and this is what they do. He wasn't trying to hurt anyone, and he did not hurt anyone. Just give him a detention and let's be done with this.

ASS. PRINCIPAL: Actually we would like to suspend him from school for a few days.

MR. BUTTS: Absolutely not! If you suspend him, he will be thrown off the baseball team!

ASS. PRINCIPAL: Seymour's actions must have serious consequences Mr. Butts.

MR. BUTTS: That is for me, his father, to decide. You will not take the baseball team away from him. He is going to get a scholarship!

ASS. PRINCIPAL: But Mr. Butts-

MR. BUTTS: Look, my best friend's wife is chair of the board of education.

ASS. PRINCIPAL: Mr. Butts-

MR. BUTTS: Just drop the issue.

ASS. PRINCIPAL: But Mr. Butts-

MR. BUTTS: It has been handled. Give him detention if you like, but this ends here.

And it did end there. Seymour was not even given detention. It was not to be discussed again.

Another fun part of the paper is that it is also published on the school's website, for anyone to comment on anonymously. I was once, in passing, asked to comment on staff reductions for an article. Soon after, an anonymous discussion about my speaking and writing skills ensued:

From: A Jaded Student

Ironic that an English teacher is quoted in here using "less" when she should be using "fewer." With illiteracy in the U.S. as high as it is, English classes should teach the English language.

27

From: Another Disenchanted Student

I am disgusted by this error. It damages her credibility as a teacher of English and thus the entire faculty and makes me feel utter embarrassment for my school.

From: A Jaded Student

It is obvious why we should learn formal grammatical and spelling conventions in school. However, literary analysis should be relegated to an elective course. Something that is merely a hobby should not be forced upon the entire student population.

To: A Jaded Student

It's completely irrelevant to point the finger at an English teacher for a grammatical error made in an informal conversation. Written and spoken word are not the same, and the teacher's words do not need to be scrutinized for grammar, but for meaning.

From: A Jaded Student

I only meant that statement to be a prelude to my main point, because it is a good depiction of my frustration with this school, its faculty and curriculum (also, I don't agree that the fact that the statement was spoken informally makes the grammar irrelevant.)

Unsurprisingly I refused to be interviewed for the paper ever again.

DINOSAURS VS. JEWS

Angus was a quiet student. I never heard anything from his corner of the room or saw anything unusual in his work until we started a unit on the Holocaust. I showed the class a documentary called *Night and Fog*. It is gruesome and has very graphic images from concentration camps, including a room with a six-foot-high pile of human hair and huge pits of rotting corpses. I don't show this film to be morbid, I show it because I know that most students do not fully understand the magnitude of genocide and some don't care. They need to be shocked into the reality of it. Apparently this film was not enough to shock Angus into caring. At the exact moment when a bulldozer pushes hundreds of lifeless bodies into a ditch, Angus let out a huge, audible yawn. When I looked at him in horror, he exclaimed, "I'm so bored!"

I tried to ignore him. I tried not to overreact. *He's just a teenager, probably looking for attention*, I told myself. Maybe this is a coping mechanism or a cry for attention. I wouldn't justify it with the big reaction he was probably looking for. I collected the students' response sheets and tried to shake off Angus' behavior. This was his response:

1.   What is your emotional reaction to the film?

I feel the same way every Holocaust film makes me feel- like I'm bored and I'm about to write an essay contrasting the protagonist and antagonist of a bad novel.

29

2.   What parts of this film are the most memorable for you?

It isn't memorable to me. I don't know why it would be. The Holocaust has been stuffed down my throat since 8th grade and I don't care. There are things that are much worse.

3.   If people in your town were being forced out of their homes because of their race or religion, what would you do?

I'd continue what I was doing, which was not caring.

He left the rest of the worksheet blank, except for a drawing of an enormous turtle with a palm tree growing on its back and a steamboat with the word "NOEL" on it.

You must be thinking that clearly we have an anti-Semite whose parents are in the KKK. Well, I assumed the same thing.

I called Angus in for a chat. I asked him why he wrote such insensitive and alarming comments. He said the same thing he wrote on his sheet, that the Holocaust is boring, and he doesn't care. I pointed out that he wrote that there are worse things in life. I asked him to name something that is worse than genocide. He said, "What about the dinosaurs? That was a whole species that was wiped out!"

He was genuinely serious about that statement. I said, "They were wiped out naturally, not by other dinosaurs or species because of their religion or skin color." He shrugged and said that he only cared about dinosaurs. I asked him if he had a problem with Jewish people. He said that he was Jewish. I was shocked. I admitted that I couldn't understand his insensitivity, being that he is Jewish himself. He said, "Well I'm only half Jewish. My mom's Jewish, and I hate her." I asked him to elaborate, and he made me promise not to call her. I reluctantly agreed, and he said that he hates his mom because she is very negative and judgmental. And because he hates his mom, he hates Jewish people and doesn't care about the Holocaust. But he really feels for the dinosaurs.

ROLLERS AND GUMPS

Every generation has its own vocabulary to which adults are oblivious. But sometimes it is critical that we know certain words, like the word "roller." This is a term used to describe a whore because she is rolling around from bed to bed, particularly adept at performing oral sex. I learned this at a staff meeting.

Maybe if we had known that this word is as explosive as the word "cunt" we would have disciplined the young man who used it consistently towards another student. But she took matters into her own hands. This ninety-pound freshman had had enough of being called a roller in the hallway every day. She brought a huge kitchen knife to school and when the gigantic senior football star called her a roller she promptly took out the knife and stabbed him, as hard as she could, in the shoulder. There was blood everywhere, splattered across the floor and lockers. This occurred right outside of my classroom. Everyone was screaming as loud as they could, and many were cheering. Another teacher ran to the boy's aid. While helping the injured student off the floor, he got blood all over himself. Several students took pictures of this and posted them on various social networks. The local news stations quickly got a hold of these images and reported that the teacher had been stabbed. His poor family didn't know what was going on for several hours.

The boy needed a lot of stitches but was ultimately okay. The girl fled the school but was eventually caught. Amazingly she was expelled from school (This is amazing because they don't usually expel students for things like this). I can't

31

help but wonder, was she not allowed back because she didn't have parents with lawyers who advocated for her right to an education? (More on this later.)

Other teenage vocabulary I have recently learned includes:

BAE (n) - Danish word for feces; term used to refer to a regular companion with whom one has a romantic or sexual relationship

Tom may be Daisy's husband, but Gatsby is (her) bae.

BAIT (n) - a person who others find extremely attractive

Kids cannot fathom how Madonna used to be the bait.

BANDO (n) - an abandoned house in an impoverished neighborhood, most often used for drug dealing, see also TRAPPIN

Harold no longer comes to school because he now devotes himself full-time to trappin out da bando.

BASIC (adj) - any person, place or activity that is unsophisticated

Only a basic student would try to slap her teacher.

BEAST (adj) - excellent; extremely impressive

This custard is beast.

BLOWN (adj) - sad or displeased because someone or something has failed to fulfill one's hopes or expectations

My scooter won't start so I'm blown.

BOOSTED (adj) - feeling deep pleasure or satisfaction; very enthusiastic and eager

Even though I failed English, I'm still going to graduate so I'm feeling rather boosted.

BOP (n) – a female who performs oral sex on many men

(v) – to perform oral sex on a man

Seymour could not get anyone to bop him due to his poor personal hygiene.

BOSS (adj) - An adjective used in many situations describing something or someone that is superior.

Analyzing English literature is boss.

BRICK (adj) - extremely cold

Make sure you wear your mittens, for it is quite brick outside.

BRUH (n) – similar to the slang term "bro," an affectionate way to refer to a friend; also used as a general declaration of being overwhelmed or exhausted, see also CUZ

After taking the Scholastic Achievement Test, I turned to my friend, threw my head back, and uttered, "Bruh."

BUST (v) - to take action in a fight; see also POP OFF

Hershel was the first person to bust during the fight.

CLAPPER (n) - a promiscuous woman (specifically describes the details of her overused private parts)

Hester Prynne was considered a clapper.

CRACKIN (adj) - fashionably attractive or stylish

Those lederhosen that Hans was wearing were crackin!

CUZ (n) - a comrade or companion, often used as a term of address, see also BRUH

Winthrop is my cuz from my days in the dormitory at Harvard.

DONK (n) - a very round, attractive pair of buttocks

Sit your donk down before I throw you out the goddamned window.

FOB (n) - short for "fresh off the boat;" an immigrant who has not lived in the country for very long

The children tried to get the FOB to say inappropriate comments in English.

GUAP (n) - a considerable amount of money

Public school teachers do not make a lot of guap.

GUH (adj) - referring to when someone/something is irritating or annoying

The rowdy students got me guh.

GUMP (n) - a coward

No one expected Fred to show up to the fight because he is a gump.

JAH (adv) - very; extremely; quite

At the end of the school year, I am jah burnt out.

JOINT (n) - general noun for any object

Can you pass me that joint? (In this case, it means pencil)

JONIN (v) - to make jokes or insults towards another person

The student wore wooden clogs and everyone was jonin on him.

LIT (adj) – impressive; favorable

When asked to describe his trip to Tibet, Franz replied with a mere word: "lit."

LOAFIN (v) - Being lazy

Students don't want to get up off the floor when they are loafin.

LUNCHING (v) - acting foolishly; to lie, sit, or stand in a relaxed or lazy way

I meant to come to the office for extra help, but instead I was lunching in the hallway.

NAH (v) - used to express dissent, denial, or refusal, as in response to a question or request; often used after "or" to obtain an answer to a pressing question

Will you be attending the inaugural ball or nah?

OG (adj) - short for "original gangster;" an older person who is still hip

I did not know that when my students said I'm OG it was a compliment.

ON FLEEK (adj) - having all the required or desirable elements, qualities, or characteristics as to be considered perfect

The winner of the National Merit Scholarship must have grades that are on fleek.

PEEP (v) – to direct one's gaze toward someone or something or in a specified direction

As I read the newspaper, my grandfather requested that I peep the scores of the latest squash championship.

POP OFF (v) - a command used to let one's opponent know that you are ready to fight; see also BUST

If you are ready to fight me, then pop off!

RATCHET (adj) - lacking good manners, refinement, or grace (of a person or their appearance or behavior); see also BASIC

The way the student was grinding her behind upon the crotches of others at the homecoming dance was truly ratchet.

SALTY (adj) - angry; upset

When students grade-grub, it gets me salty.

SICE (v) – to cause strong feelings of enthusiasm and eagerness

The pending break had the students siced.

SIDE JOINT (n) – person with whom one engages in intercourse with outside of their main relationship (the official sexual partner or spouse would be referred to as the "main joint")

Abigail was John Proctor's side joint.

SMASH (v) - have sexual intercourse

If a man smashes a lot of girls he is a stud, but a woman is considered a roller.

SNEAK DIS (v) - to insult someone's character or appearance in a sneaky or sarcastic way

I cannot help but sneak dis my students who have names such as Sha'Nationality.

SPRUNG (adj) - deeply in love; obsessed

Gatsby was sprung for Daisy.

SQUAD (n) - an informal group of individuals who share the same interests

The English Department is my squad.

SWEET (adj) - a weak, feminine, or homosexual male

Just because my boyfriend wears my panties doesn't mean he's sweet.

THIRSTY (adj) - Having keen interest or intense desire

Myrtle Wilson was so thirsty in that scene.

THE PLUG (n) – A supplier of illegal substances

I was shocked to learn that Mortimer was the plug for the entire school.

THOT (n) - acronym for "that hoe over there;" characterized by or having numerous sexual partners on a casual basis; see also CLAPPER

Abigail Williams was nothing but a cheap thot.

TRAPPIN (v) - The act of dealing or selling illegal drugs for the accumulation of wealth (The TRAP is the place where the drugs are sold)

Harold no longer comes to school because he now devotes himself full time to trappin out da bando.

THROWING SHADE (v) - To publicly denounce or disrespect

Some people throw shade at the government's failure to provide an adequate and permanent healthcare system for all of its citizens.

TURNT (adj) - a state of altered consciousness induced by alcohol or narcotics

The student was so turnt that he could barely open his eyes.

UNK (n) - Usually refers to a crack addict; can also be used when talking to someone with "crack head" characteristics or tendencies

When you have an argument with yourself, you look like an unk.

YEET (n) - Term used to express excitement

Only 20 years until retirement! Yeet!

ENOUGH TO BE HORRIFYING

Geraldine was awake for most of the class on this particular day but was staring endlessly into her lap. I figured she was on her phone or doing work for another class so I asked her several times to pick her head up. She responded for a moment, and then returned to whatever was so interesting in her crotch. Finally, I walked over to her and saw that she had cut her wrists with a pair of dull scissors. The cuts were not really deep, but deep enough to be horrifying. I gasped, and demanded that she go to the nurse. She shook her head no. I told another student to walk her to the nurse and Geraldine got up and reluctantly left the room. She returned to school the next day, and I never heard about the incident again. When I inquired about her mental health, I was told that it was confidential information and that she was fine.

THE GIANT, WRITHING PETRI DISH

When I was interning, my supervisor gave me a piece of advice for my first year. "Don't ever be absent in your first year, even if you have to crawl to work," he told me. Those words really stuck with me, but I wonder if he had ever seen anyone get as sick as I got in my first year.

My body had been used to somewhat sanitary conditions for the previous four years. While college dorms are not the most sterile of environments, they are cleaned regularly and have a small percentage of people walking the halls at one time. Other than traveling on an airplane a few times, my immune system hadn't been given much of a challenge until I started working at a school with thousands of teenagers. I washed my hands constantly and carried a can of Lysol like a concealed weapon, but it didn't prevent me from getting two Clostridium difficile infections (better known as C diff). C. diff is a bacterial infection of the colon that causes symptoms ranging from diarrhea to life-threatening inflammation of the colon. It certainly *felt* life threatening.

It started with severe abdominal pain one night and became so intense that I fainted. It also involved defecating blood. After a battery of tests in the ER, they informed me that I had contracted a bacterial infection that is almost always caught from working in a hospital or nursing home. I assured them that I had not been to either recently. I said that I work in a huge school and they insisted that

I must have been in a hospital or nursing home to catch such a severe case. Nope, I realized, I just work in a giant, writhing petri dish. Although they said it was very unlikely that I would suffer from the same infection twice, one month later I found myself bleeding into the toilet yet again. I thought about what my supervising teacher said about crawling to work and I decided that an inflamed colon was a good enough reason to take the day off.

Stress is obviously a major contributing factor to a weakened immune system, and the average person's immune system has never experienced stress like that of an American high school teacher. I once worked with an intern who claimed to have an immune system of steel. She maintained that she hadn't had a cold since she was a little kid. In her second week of student teaching, she developed what looked like a pimple on her lip. She ignored it but it kept getting bigger and bigger until one morning she woke up with a boil the size of a golf ball hanging off of her bottom lip. It turned out to be a Staph infection, which apparently 25% of the human population carries in their mouth, nose, genitals and anus.*

In my first year, there was another first-year teacher who took the "never miss a day" thing very seriously. She fought very hard to make it through one particularly difficult day. She was extremely dizzy, had the chills and sweats at the same time, and terrible abdominal pain. She looked at her desk and could barely understand the paperwork. Her mind was so fuzzy that she couldn't come up with the lesson plan for the day or even make something else up. Driving home was very difficult. She couldn't concentrate. It turned out that she had gotten an intestinal parasite.

I was never a chronic hand washer, but after my first year of teaching I became obsessed with washing my hands and spraying all surfaces with Lysol. I even spray the general vicinity of particularly germy students. I may have dry hands, but at least I haven't had any parasites recently.

Perhaps it was the stress of her students drawing pictures of her and writing "fugly" underneath it that weakened her immunity.

A.D.D. A.K.A. THE GET OUT OF WORK

FREE CARD

According to U.S. Centers for Disease Control and Prevention data, approximately 11 percent of school-age children in the United States -- and 19 percent of high-school-age boys -- have been diagnosed with attention-deficit/hyperactivity disorder. Of the 150 students I teach in completely mainstream (not special education or inclusion) classes, about 20% have been diagnosed with attention deficit disorder or attention deficit hyperactivity disorder, which is right on target with the CDC's statistics.

Each student with an A.D.D. or A.D.H.D. diagnosis receives special accommodations to put them on an equal playing field with the other students, including extended time for homework, tests, papers, projects, etc. Most also have a right to preferential seating. They are also entitled to special notes that I am supposed to prepare for them in their preferred formats (like charts). I don't have a problem with this, for those students who actually have this disorder. But I can't help but feel that A.D.D. is becoming an excuse for many other things and it is getting way out of hand.

Many other students in my mainstream classes have a 504 Plan, which means they have been identified as having some kind of learning disability and get certain accommodations in class, such as textbooks that have been pre-highlighted, extended time on tests and assignments, a peer note taker, a preferred schedule and teacher selection, personal teacher check-ins, written step-by-step instructions, reduction in workload, frequent breaks, alternative reading materials, alternative testing formats such as verbal exams etc. The most common disability my students have that require these accommodations, besides A.D.D., is Executive Functioning Disorder. This is defined as an inefficiency in planning, organization, strategizing, paying attention to and remembering details, and managing time and space. I would imagine many teenagers would qualify for this disability if tested.

Keep in mind, again, that I am not a special education teacher and I do not teach inclusion classes (Inclusion classes have mainstream students mixed with special ed. students. There is both a subject teacher and a special ed. teacher in the room). I teach "regular" English classes and I have no formal or informal training to handle students with special needs.

I get daily emails from parents reminding me that their child has A.D.D. or E.F.D. and will need a lot of extra time on an assignment, or will need to redo something they did poorly on because they have A.D.D. and need more chances to get it right.

During Back to School Night I had a parent literally corner me in the five minutes I have between classes (which I usually spend shaking hands with parents). She said the following, "My son Chuck has A.D.D. so he won't be handing in most of his homework." She said this quite forcefully, as though I had to agree. Before I could answer her, she said, "Chuck is extremely gifted so he needs a lot of extra help. But don't expect him to do any homework, you know, because of his A.D.D." I just nodded and said, "Oh okay." After that little interaction I didn't expect Chuck to do homework, so when I entered all those zeros into the grade book it wasn't a surprise to me. But it was quite a surprise to Chuck's mom who promptly emailed me asking what all the zeros were for. Let's just say she had to speak to the administration, because she felt those zeros shouldn't count against her gifted son's grade. Chuck, by the way, was generally too stoned to even lift his head off the desk.

41

On the first day of school one year, I received the following letter in my mailbox:

Dear Teachers,

My name is Vlad and I'll be your student this year. I like to let my teachers know that I have Asperger's syndrome and what that means. According to Wikipedia, Asperger's is one of the autism spectrum disorders or pervasive developmental disorders, which are a spectrum of psychological conditions that are characterized by abnormalities of social interaction and communication that pervade the individual's functioning, by restricted and repetitive interests and behavior. Here is a list of the specific symptoms that I might demonstrate in class:

● General social skills: I want to socialize but I do not understand how to interact.

● Relating to others: I do not understand emotions or how to use social cues accurately in a group situation. I may not understand if an activity or conversation is upsetting to another person and I will probably state that I find the activity boring or stupid.

● Difficulty working with others: I may not understand how to interact with my peers or how to play by common social rules. I generally cannot do group work because I end up arguing with everyone.

● Problems with two-way conversation: I have trouble with initiating and maintaining a two-way conversation. I may appear to talk at someone rather than with him. I can seem angry too but I'm not. Conversation topics may focus on my obsessive interests, like wizardry. I also speak inappropriately, often too loudly, but I don't know it.

● Inability to understand common social cues: I may not comprehend common "social cues" such as facial expressions, body language or gestures. If you do something physically to show that you are upset, I won't know.

● Rigid range of interests for social interaction: I will only engage in a narrow range of activities or talk about certain subjects, like wizardry. I also avoid eye contact.

• Inappropriate responses: I may behave or respond to social situations in an unusual or inappropriate manner. For example, I once laughed really hard when another student said that she had an abortion.

I hope that I'll get an A in your class.

Sincerely,

Vlad

While I commend Vlad for being a self-advocate, I wasn't exactly excited to teach a kid who might laugh at someone for getting an abortion. Another student I'll call "Chouie" had A.D.D. and never followed directions. Regardless of the task (an essay, a multiple choice quiz, a journal), he would do something completely different. Sometimes he would just make up an assignment instead of doing the one I assigned. His parents were very upset that he was failing the class. We all had a meeting and his counselor and case worker told me to grade whatever he gave me. I explained that he wasn't doing what he was supposed to do, so I had no way to grade him. "Grade him based on whatever assignment he is doing then," they said. "How do I do that?" I asked. "I didn't create the assignment, so I do not have a basis for assessment."

"Grade his work as if you did assign it," they replied. "It's not his fault that he can't follow the directions. He has A.D.D."

Apparently A.D.D. makes it difficult to even *see* parts of the test. On more than one occasion, I have had students who missed entire parts of a test and blamed it on their A.D.D. One student emailed me to ask why he ended up with a D on the final exam, and I informed him that he did not complete one of the essays. "That's not fair," he wrote. "I didn't even see it! You took off thirty points but it wasn't my fault." After a parent got involved, I had to let the student write the essay weeks later and adjust his grade.

A.D.D. is also exacerbated by anxiety, so I am told to avoid certain situations which might cause uneasiness for certain students. For example, I received a notice from the Special Education Department that I ·could not, under any circumstances, grade a specific student's work with red ink. Red ink made the student very nervous and added to her A.D.D. I made sure to always grade that student's work in purple or green ink.

According to several online sources such as WebMD.com, the symptoms of Attention Deficit Disorder are: careless mistakes and lack of attention to details; lack of persistent attention; poor listening skills; failure to always follow through on tasks; poor organizational skills; avoidance of tasks requiring sustained mental effort; losing things; and being easily distracted and forgetful in daily activities.

For the hyperactive/impulsive type the symptoms are fidgeting and squirming; need to leave seat; difficulty with silent activities; too much talking; blurting out responses; unable to wait turn, and being invasive. If you recall being a teenager or have recently lived or worked with one, you would probably agree that these descriptions are generally indicative of simply being a teenager, which is a tad confusing. Do they all have this disorder or are some more teenager-like than others?

Another disorder that seems to encompass general teenage behavior is referred to as "Oppositional Defiant Disorder." This is defined as "a condition in which a child displays an ongoing pattern of uncooperative, defiant, hostile, and annoying behavior toward people in authority." If you have ever lived with a teenager, you will probably recognize this behavior as normal. I have had students with this classification who require special allowances for generally disrespectful and outrageous behavior.

For example, I had a student who turned in the following essay during the first week of school:

I have been asked to write about the message behind the book I read this summer but I cannot and will not do that because the message is right there in the title. The book is an autobiography. It is about someone's life. Somehow the people who came up with this prompt expect me to write a 4-5 paragraph essay analyzing the meaning of an autobiography. Since there were only three options for books to read this summer, you should have looked at the prompt and realized that it is dumb and does not work. The story teaches about the life and work of the author AND NOTHING ELSE.

The book talks about the author's childhood, having his family broken up, racism, a love for dance, avoiding the draft, being a traveling salesman and going to prison. It talks about Islam. There is no message.

You know what? I cannot keep up with this charade. Forget which person I am supposed to be talking in, I am now talking directly to YOU, the teacher. Why did you choose this prompt? Seriously. This book does not work for this fucking prompt but you went ahead and gave it the all clear. Nevermind the fact that it calls itself an autobiography when it isn't even written by the author. That is stupid but still doesn't make the prompt you chose work. Did you even read the book we had to read? How hard would it have been to make a prompt that works for this book? You could have easily made a writing prompt that works for all three books.

I am willing to accept that I may be murdering my grade by breaking "standard essay-writing procedures" and not talking in the correct "person" and getting "off topic," but I literally managed to write nothing about this topic. I am yelling at you on this paper essentially to fill up space and have enough paragraphs.

Maybe I have missed some deep, hidden meaning in the book but I find that hard to believe. Maybe other people who read this book are able to pull an answer out of their ass but I cannot. I would like to see where this honest response gets me. I may be ruining my grade and becoming a problem child but I have stood by and will always stand by the fact that this is the dumbest writing prompt that I have ever been asked to complete.

I was inclined to give this student a zero for making no attempt to answer the prompt and being rude and disrespectful. But I was told that I must allow him a second chance to rewrite it and I must also help him rewrite it because he did not fully understand the prompt. All of these accommodations had to be made due to his Oppositional Defiant Disorder and A.D.D.

Another student once made a racist remark to another student. When I spoke to him about it after class his only response was, "Well, you know I have been diagnosed with Oppositional Defiant Disorder." I didn't realize that included racism.

CAN I ASK YOU A QUESTION?

Reader, can I ask you a question?

Do you have any idea what it's like to have to continually repeat yourself? It can drive a person mad. Can I ask you a question? Do you have any idea what it's like to have to constantly repeat yourself? It makes you question reality. Do you have any idea what it's like to have to repeat yourself? You start to wonder, is this really happening? Do you have any idea what it's like to always have to repeat yourself? It makes anger boil up in every part of your body. Do you have any idea what it's like to have to constantly repeat yourself?

IT CAN MAKE YOU FEEL LIKE YOU ARE LOSING YOUR MIND.

Especially when everyone reacts to your reaction as though it is a massive *over*reaction, because they have not been listening either, and do not understand that this is the tenth time you have had to repeat a simple command.

Take, for example, this modest request: "Please open your books to page 57." It is understandable that a few students may not have heard you. They ask, "What page?" and you repeat, "Page 57."

But then another student asks what page we are on and then another. You have now repeated the page number four separate times. So you write the number on the board along with the words, "We are on page..." to alleviate any confusion in the future. The class starts reading. Another student, who has been busy texting

46

on his phone, yells out, "Yo! What page!" You point to the board. The student opens to page 57 and examines it and interrupts the person reading with, "No we ain't!" You take a deep breath and respond, "We *began* on page 57 and now we have moved on to page 58."

You continue reading. Another student awakens from his drool-soaked desk. He does not think to ask a neighbor what page we are on, or to open the book and find out for himself. He does not look at the board. Instead, he calls out, "What page are we on!" You drop your book and exclaim, "Are you kidding me! You have got to be kidding me! Why don't you ask someone else instead of interrupting the whole class?" The students look at you like you are an escaped mental patient. One responds with, "Yo Miss, you got *no* chill."

Another adds, "Yeah, he was just asking what page we're on so he can read along."

Do you have any idea what it's like to have to constantly repeat yourself? If not, be thankful.

THOUGHTFUL GIFTS

I asked a group of teachers for a list of the strangest gifts they have ever received from students. Here are my personal favorites:

- A Dollar Store mug and candy combo with "World's Greatest Lover" on it

- A gift card for a bikini wax

- A pair of fur-covered handcuffs for the teacher to use with her "Beyoncé" (fiancé)

- #1 Lover mug

- Used hair gel

- A foil rose that was actually a red lace thong *(Students mistakenly buy this gift for teachers a lot.)*

- A kindergartener gave her teacher a perfume called "Sexy Thang"

- A pack of hangers

- A sympathy card… for the holidays

- 3 razors, a chapstick, a toothbrush and a pencil wrapped in a rubber band

- Karma Sutra cologne

- Perfume and sexy underwear so the teacher can "Make her *own* baby!"

- Pink lace panties from a 3rd grader

- Chocolates that a student admitted her dad stole from the Dollar Tree

- A copy of American Psycho wrapped in newspaper

- A gift card to a liquor store

- A gift bag with grapefruit and appetite suppressants

- A box of panty liners

- Cellulite cream

THE SPAWN OF HELICOPTER PARENTS

While there is a primary focus on students who bully in schools right now, there are few published studies on parents and students who bully teachers. Research shows that a fifth of teachers have been abused online by students or their parents.[1] In most of these cases absolutely nothing was done, even the incidents that were reported to police were ignored. It is almost like teachers are expected to accept a bit of bullying as part of their job description.

When people wonder why the retention rate for teachers is so poor, they rarely consider bullying. A major survey of teachers conducted by the American Psychological Association revealed that 7% of teachers in the U.S. are threatened with physical violence from parents or students and 3% are actually physically attacked. Females are actually harassed more than twice as much as male teachers.[2]

More than one in three teachers has been on the receiving end of online/cyberbullying from both students and parents in the U.K. Hundreds of teachers were surveyed nationwide and 35% said that either they, or their colleagues, had been subjected to some form of online abuse, ranging from postings on Facebook, Instagram, and Twitter. While most of the abuse came from students, in more than a quarter of cases parents were the abusers.

When parents bully teachers their kids learn that it is okay to treat teachers with disrespect. In 2008, Katherine Evans, a Florida high school student, was disciplined for cyberbullying a teacher on Facebook. She created a group called "Ms. Sarah Phelps is the worst teacher I've ever met!" and featured a picture of the teacher, and a request for other students to "express your feelings of hatred." The school suspended the student for three days for "disruptive behavior" and for "Bullying/Cyberbullying Harassment towards a staff member." In response, the student filed a lawsuit against the principal for violating her right to free speech. The suit went to the Florida Supreme Court and the student won, which translated to awarding of financial damages for lawyer fees and the suspension being wiped from her permanent record.[3]

A 12th-grade student in Pennsylvania named Justin Layshock was suspended for 10 days after creating a fake Myspace profile of his principal. The profile listed the principal's birthday as "too drunk to remember." For the physical description, he wrote "big," as the principal is a rather large man. It also said that he smokes "big cigs" and thinks the words "too damn big" when he first wakes up. The profile, along with many nasty comments added by other students quickly went viral. The school traced the profile to 17-year-old Layshock, who confessed and apologized. They suspended him for 10 days and then transferred him to an alternative education program. The punishment led to an ACLU lawsuit. The school eventually let Layshock return to school. On July 10, 2007, a federal judge ruled that the school's suspension had been unconstitutional and ordered a trial to decide whether the student was permitted to compensatory damages for the school district's violation of his First Amendment rights. In February 2010, a three-judge panel of the Third Circuit of Appeals ruled that the school district had violated Layshock's First Amendment free speech rights. The school district appealed the ruling to the U.S. Supreme Court but they declined to hear the case.[4]

Justin Swidler, a 14-year-old from Pennsylvania, created a website called "Teacher Sux" in which he ridiculed Principal Thomas Kartsotis and math teacher Kathleen Fulmer. The site included animated images of the principal getting hit by a slow-moving bullet, and an image of the math teacher morphing into a picture of Adolf Hitler. One part of the website called, "Why should she die?" gave several reasons the math teacher should be killed, followed by a request

51

for money. "Take a good look at the diagram and the reasons I give, then give me $20 to help pay for the hit man," the website said. The school district contacted the local police and the F.B.I. Both declined to press criminal charges against the student although there was clearly a threat made against the teacher.[5]

At a high school near my home, a group of kids recently edited a Wikipedia entry so that it falsely stated that a teacher had been arrested for possession of crystal meth and child pornography. The entry was up for about three weeks, during which time many students, parents and local people of influence were directed to read its content. While the content was removed, there was no investigation into who wrote the slanderous material. The teacher still suffers a public backlash from parents who are now suspicious of his character.

In another case, a teacher reported receiving a large number of phone calls and emails from gay men soliciting him for sex. It turned out that a student had posted the teacher's name and contact information on a gay sex website. There was no way of tracing who had done this.

Another incident involved a parent filming a teacher's ass during a class show after which he put the clip online with Van Halen's song "Hot for Teacher" playing in the background. No charges were filed against the parent.

In my school, a student photoshopped a young female teacher's head onto the body of a naked model. It looked quite real. He passed out hundreds of copies in the hallway at school. The teacher was so devastated that she left the teaching profession for a few years but eventually came back.

I am not saying that students are not entitled to free speech. I just want people to be aware of the levels of disrespect that teachers endure and the lack of consequences.

Just like adults, kids have a very public forum online to express their opinions about whatever they choose. Yet unlike many adults, they lack the tact and ability to think critically about the impact their comments can have. Take for example the website called ratemyteachers.com. This is a very popular site where anyone in the world can look up a teacher by name or by school and see what people have posted anonymously about them. It not only rates their performance but it rates their popularity. Until recently it actually rated their "hotness" as well. The site also gives anyone the chance to comment on a teacher's performance with absolutely no filter. You are not required to log in or enter your name or email address to post a comment. Ratemyteachers.com has over 15 million ratings for more than 11 million teachers.

According to the site, all comments are reviewed and approved by volunteer moderators to ensure they are consistent with the site's rules or guidelines before they are posted on the website. I'm not sure who is moderating and what they are removing because it seems that you can pretty much write whatever you like and it will appear shortly after. This site and websites like it give young people, who lack the maturity and discretion to be able to properly rate their educators, a place to be angry and inappropriate. Thankfully, I have only been rated a few times and they are mostly positive comments. But I have very hardworking and dedicated co-workers who have been decimated on this website.

For example, a very devoted teacher who typically stays at school until 8 o'clock at night grading papers and working on lesson plans has gotten several nasty comments because she is a "hard grader." Kids have written the following remarks: "She is rude and picks on students just to satisfy her horrible heart; she is useless as a teacher; worst teacher I've ever had, our whole class hates her; she manages to say nothing understandable in an hour; I have no respect for her; the work is stupid and she is stupid; a terrible teacher and a terrible person; should be in a mental asylum." Whether or not these statements are true, it is unfair for students to be able to say such abusive things and have it stay on the internet forever. When you Google a teacher's name you are almost sure to find quotes from ratemyteachers.com on the front page, which can impact a person's career and life forever. Many students write absolutely nothing productive and merely express their emotions towards the teacher as an individual such as, "I dislike you highly; I hate her with a fiery passion; total female dog;" or just "I hate you." Some teachers are called morons, idiots, senile or simply told to shut up. But even worse are the violent threats that are made. In 2010, a student commented that "at the end of the year, I'm setting her (teacher) on fire," while another student said, "I would take so much pleasure in killing this woman."[6]

What can be even more hurtful than threats are the sexual comments a teacher receives. A former coworker of mine is gorgeous. Her ratings include comments such as, "She's like really pretty; she's the bait (slang for sexy); so hawt (hot), etc." This really embarrasses her. Her online ratings aren't the only inappropriate things she encounters. She gets disgusting anonymous emails from students that describe what they want to do to her. She even had students throw condoms at her when she turned around to write on the board. Sadly, yet not surprisingly, she is one of the 50% of teachers who left the profession.

Many organizations have asked for this site to be taken down, including the National Union of Teachers in the U.K. and New York State United Teachers (NYSUT). In the U.S. and U.K., the request was denied on free speech grounds, yet in France the courts ruled in favor of the teachers' unions. The decision was made after citing "incitement to public disorder."[7] The education minister "totally supported teachers whose difficult mission will not be the object of anonymous attacks on the internet."[8]

On a side note, there is also a college and graduate school version of this website called ratemyprofessor.com. While you would think this would be a website with more mature options for rating one's professor, there is still the chance to rate your professor's hotness. If they receive a certain amount of hotness votes, they actually get a little hot tamale icon next to their name in their school's listing of professors. According to the website, "Choosing the best courses and professors is a rite of passage for every student, and connecting with peers on the site has become a key way for millions of students to navigate this process." Clearly, whether or not a professor is "hot" is an essential part of the course selection process.

While the site itself may not be very mature, one can assume that the level of ratings and comments would be, since the audience is older and seemingly wiser than middle and high school students. Yet the comments often have the same immature and abusive tone, they are just more creative and well written. For example, a former English professor of mine received the following comment,

"There's just something off about him that I can't put my finger on. He smiles, but there's no warmth there. Just a terrible emptiness like you'd find in the rusting hull of a ship forgotten at the bottom of a dead sea. Something must have happened to him to make him this way." While my former professor might find this comment hurtful, I'm sure the "he's super sexy" comment would make up for it.

Many students choose to speak directly to the professor on this site, although they still remain anonymous. A student wrote the following to a professor, "Get over yourself. You teach below average and this nation needs more than mediocre teachers. Sheesh, deflate that ego and look in the mirror. A speck of dust in the universe..." Now maybe this woman has pretty tough skin and wouldn't let this bother her. But she'd have to be made of stone to let the following comment roll off of her: "You should see this woman naked. Take her class then ask her out, she'll go for it, always does."

While many people may think that these websites are not taken seriously and are merely a place for disgruntled students to vent, they are in fact taken quite seriously, by students choosing classes, parents and even schools during the hiring process. A student commented that "Anyone who would enroll in this professor's class after consulting rate my professor is either a social misfit or a psychopath. It's like jumping in front of a train although you saw it coming." And he or she is not in the minority. A student reporter for Santa Clara University states that, "Many of my peers would tell me how they chose a class solely based on the ratings a teacher received on the website or how easy or difficult a teacher was judged to be. I found it surprising and somewhat scary that people would take comments on an anonymous website so seriously."[9]

Besides students taking the reviews so seriously, some administrators do as well. A math teacher claims that he had a principal who felt that this website was a valid part of the teacher's personnel folder. The teachers all went online and promptly became brilliant teachers by anonymously rating themselves several times. It was after the students wrote scathing reviews of the principal that she finally decided to reconsider. Another teacher was actually asked about his ratings during an interview for a teaching position.

Sites like Rate My Teacher are basically forums for cyberbullying. Recently, three Eastern Michigan University professors had no idea that while they were teaching they were being verbally attacked by the Honors College students sitting in their class. Students shared nasty comments on their phones via Yik Yak, a smartphone application that lets people anonymously post brief comments on virtual bulletin boards. Since the app appeared in November 2013, it has been causing chaos in schools as a result of students' posting violent threats, racial slurs, and malicious gossip. At the end of the class, a student pulled one of the professors aside and showed her a record of the comments the students were making during her class. They had written more than 100 disparaging posts, "including sexual remarks, references to them using 'bitch' and a vulgar term for female anatomy, and insults about their appearance and teaching."[10] After class, one of the professors sent emails with screenshots of some of the worst messages to university officials, urging them to take some sort of action. "I have been defamed, my reputation besmirched. I have been sexually harassed and verbally abused," she wrote. "I am about ready to hire a lawyer." The school responded by cancelling the class. They felt the comments students were making showed the unpopularity of the course and the professors who taught it and removed it from the course offerings. There was no investigation into the comments that were made.

Threats of violence towards teachers can get even worse than that. In her book *Hate Crimes in Cyberspace*, Danielle Keats Citron, a professor at the University of Maryland's School of Law, discusses Yik Yak posts from students about their teachers. One disturbing post she had seen referenced a lecture by another professor. "It said, 'If this woman doesn't stop talking, I'm going to rape her,'" Ms. Citron recounted. "As these threads popped up, once these rape conversations started, it got worse. It got more graphic."[11]

But even without harmful sites and apps like this, due to the easy anonymity of the internet, cyberbullying of teachers is inevitable. For example, students will often make a fake email through Yahoo or Gmail and send anonymous comments to teachers. As a teacher of 12th grade English, I have one of the only classes that might prevent a student from graduating. In their senior year, many students simply stop coming to school. If they fail most of their classes, they will still graduate, but English is a requirement for graduation. Thus, it is perceived to be under my jurisdiction whether or not a failing student will graduate, and not the responsibility of the student. Students who realize that they are not going to graduate too late in the semester often become infuriated and harass the teacher. They see the teacher as the one thing that is holding them back from graduation. While they can't threaten you to pass them anonymously, they get their revenge in other ways. It was during this exact situation that a colleague had a huge "F" scraped into the hood of his car.

During graduation, I saw a student who had failed my class walk across the stage. A few days later I received an email from an anonymous source that read, "Fuck you! I graduated! You stupid bitch!"

If you're thinking, "It wasn't like that in school when I was growing up," or "It wasn't like that when I was a teacher," you may not realize how dramatically things have changed in the last few years. Parents feel more entitled than ever, and they are raising their kids to be extremely entitled as well. A former director of the Parents' Program at Cornell University has studied what is referred to as "helicopter parenting." Her research shows that this type of behavior started to appear on college campuses in the 1990s. "College admissions offices began to complain that parents insisted on sitting in on their child's admission interview. Some admissions officials started to suspect that parents of prospective students wrote their essays." She states that overbearing parents have become a huge problem for colleges and universities.[12] Wealthier parents may even pay to have someone write their kid's college application essay for them. We are talking about an essay that is typically one to two pages in length, and is meant to show evidence of the student's writing ability, personality and values. According to the Common Application, an organization used by more than 500 universities to facilitate the application process, the purpose of the personal essay is to "help you distinguish yourself in your own voice."[13] It is ironic (and outrageous) that some students have someone else write this for them.

One summer I had a job at a test prep organization "helping" rising high school seniors with their college applications and mainly, their essays. I was told that I would be helping students generate a topic and editing their essays.

Although it felt a tad unethical, as long as the student did the majority of the work I felt it was okay. But I dealt with kids who couldn't or wouldn't write anything, or wrote very poorly, and no matter how much I tried to push them in the right direction, at the end of the day, this was what they were capable of. But I was told that if a student couldn't or wouldn't write, I would need to just do it for them.

Clearly these kids had everything done for them their whole lives. And now I was going to write their college application essays (which are supposed to be about meaningful experiences they've had which have shaped who they are as human beings), and all because their parents had money... Enough to pay $250 an hour for this service (of which I only received about 15%)!

Some parents will even escort their son or daughter to a job interview, call a manager to ask why their kid didn't get the job, and call to campaign for a higher salary for their child.[14]

If a parent is willing to call their adult child's workplace to advocate for them, it is no surprise that they had harassed teachers and administration until they got what they felt their child deserved. It is a cycle of never-ending entitlement that leads to mediocrity. It starts with a parent pestering a teacher to get an undeserved grade for their child. Then they manipulate their kid's way into college, or they get into college with grades they didn't earn. Next, when the kid gets a job for skills and education that look good on paper but weren't actually merited, they end up losing their job. And so far, parents cannot save a kid from being fired for poor work performance... at least not yet.

CLASSROOM EXCHANGES

(You just can't make this shit up)

ME: Does anyone else have any questions? Yes Bea, go ahead.

BEA: What have you been eating lately?

ME: Excuse me?

BEA: Have you been eating a lot of junk food?

ME: What does this have to do with anything?

BEA: It's just that you look like you're putting on a lot of weight, so I was just wondering what you've been eating.

ME: That's not appropriate Bea. Please go into the hallway.

BEA: But you asked if we had any questions, so I asked a question.

ME: I don't care Bea, that question is not appropriate. Go into the hallway.

BEA: *Okay*, I was just curious.

ME: What do you think the character's motivation was for-

CECIL: This book sucks.

ME: Well maybe if you would actually *read* the book…

CECIL: Well maybe if you would actually *read my dick*…

ME: Cecil get out.

CECIL: Okay.

No, Cecil didn't get in trouble for this, by the way.

ME: Does anyone have any questions before I hand out the test?

GILBERT: Yeah I have a question.

ME: Okay, go ahead.

GILBERT: How come you never wear tight shirts?

ME: What kind of question is that?

GILBERT: You're always wearing these shirts that look like what pregnant ladies wear. Why don't you ever wear anything tight?

ME: That's not an appropriate question. And this is what's in style!

ME: Tell me, what is your version of the American dream?

JUANITA: What's *your* American dream, Ms. Morris?

ME: It's being here with all of you Juanita.

GIUSEPPE: Yeah, right. Don't you want money? Teachers make like no money.

ME: We make enough to survive.

GIUSEPPE: How much do you make?

ME: That's private.

SHEILA: Actually your salary is considered public information since you are a public servant.

ME: What?

SHEILA: (*to the class*) You can just go on the school district's webpage and look up her salary.

GIUSEPPE: Really? Cool!

ME: Good, go ahead. I don't care. Can we get back to the discussion I was trying to have?

Five minutes later

ME: So how do you think the American dream has evolved from the 1950s to today?

GIUSEPPE: (*having just looked up my salary on his phone under his desk*) How many years have you been teaching?

ME: This is my first year. Why?

GIUSEPPE: That's not bad loot, but I'd need a lot more, like enough to get-

ME: Did you just look up my salary?

ESTHER: How much she make?

ME: Don't even think about saying it.

SHEILA: But it's public information.

ME: Yes, I know Shelia. I just don't think we need to discuss it right now. This is very disrespectful.

GIUSEPPE: Why?

ESTHER: Yeah, why? I'll tell you what I make at Target. I been a cashier for two years and they just bumped me up to-

ME: That's not the point.

GIUSEPPE: I make a lot of dough mowing lawns in the summer. And after school I clean stuff at the old people home. They pay me almost ten an hour.

ME: That's good. I'm glad.

GIUSEPPE: But if I was your age, I'd need to make a lot more than that.

ESTHER: Than *what*? How much?

BO: Just tell us already.

Giuseppe whispers to Esther, who announces my salary to the class.

BO: That's a lot of money!

SHEILA: No it's not! That's like, nothing. My dad makes like fifty times more than that.

ME: Alright I've had it. Take out your books and silently read Act 2.

ME: So who is "The Lord of the Flies?"

BALKI: Your mom.

ME Really? The lord of the flies is my mom?

BALKI: Yup.

ME: I don't think that's possible. My mom has never even left the East Coast, and the story takes place on an island in a remote region of the Pacific Ocean.

BALKI: Yeah, whatever. It's your mom.

ME: Plus, this book was published around the time my mom was born. So was she like an infant version of the lord of the flies?

BALKI: Yup.

ME: Great. Thanks for clarifying.

ME: Are there any questions before we start the test?

MORDECHAI: Is it considered inappropriate for a student to ask a teacher about their sex life?

ME: Yes, extremely inappropriate.

MORDECHAI: Never mind.

ME: Okay everyone. Take out your journals so I can give you homework points.

OTTO: Wait, what do you mean? We get points for this?

ME: Yes, as I explained last class, your first assignment is merely to bring in a journal.

OTTO: And we get points for that?

ME: Yes, because I'm sick of students not having their journals.

OTTO: So if I don't have it then I get a zero?

ME: Yes.

OTTO: But that's bullshit.

ME Excuse me?

OTTO: This is *bullshit*.

ME: Okay, you need to leave the class.

OTTO: (*standing up and speaking to the class*) Don't you guys think this is bullshit?

RUFUS: Dude, sit down.

OTTO: No. This is bullshit. She can't give me a zero for not having my notebook!

ME: Otto, leave right now. Go to your administrator.

OTTO: Good. I'm gonna tell her about this bullshit.

Otto leaves and comes back ten minutes later. He throws a paper onto my desk, gets his stuff, and walks out. The paper is from the administrator saying that he was switched into another English class.

ME: Tell me about a song that had powerful words. How did it change you?

BERNIE: The lyrics to Macklemore's song "Same Love" changed me because he said that he thought he was gay in third grade but then realized he's not.

FRUMA: You can't realize you're gay and then change your mind.

BERNIE: Yes you can.

EARLINE: It's not that hard to figure out. If you *like dick* then you're gay!

ME: Okay that's enough. That was super inappropriate.

CARLITO: Yo, what'd she just say? I wasn't listening.

ME: Nothing. Let's move on.

WILFRED: Dude, she said if you like to suck dick then you're a fag!

EARLINE: That's not what I said. You don't have to have-

CARLITO: That's hilarious! If you like sucking dick… ahahahaha!

ME: Alright, all of you get out.

ME: Hello everyone. Welcome to 11th grade English.

MELVIN: Shit.

ME: Umm… did you just curse?

MELVIN: No.

ME: Okay… so as I was saying, welcome to 11th grade English. This semester we will be focusing on-

MELVIN: Fuck.

ME: Excuse me, what is your name?

MELVIN: Melvin.

ME: Okay Melvin, what is going on here?

MELVIN: I have Tourette's.

ME: Really?

MELVIN: Yeah. Slut cunt.

ME: Oh my god! You need to go out into the hallway.

MELVIN: But it's not my fault, I have Tourette's. Bitch ass!

ME: Go into the hallway immediately.

Melvin goes into the hallway, and after I get the class working on an assignment, I go outside with my phone and call his mother. She confirms my suspicion that he did not have Tourette's syndrome.

LUDWIG: Can you help me? I don't understand these directions.

ME: Okay. It's pretty straight forward. Just write whether you agree or disagree with each statement and then explain why.

LUDWIG: Oh okay.

Five minutes later

LUDWIG: What are we supposed to be doing right now?

ME: We're working on the worksheet I just explained to you.

LUDWIG: Oh. But what are the directions?

ME: Ludwig, are you serious? I just explained this to you, plus the directions are at the top of the page.

LUDWIG: Oh yeah. Never mind.

Two minutes later

LUDWIG: I'm sorry Ms. Morris, but I'm just too drunk to do this worksheet.

Note: It is 8 o'clock in the morning.

Loretta, who is 15 years old and nine months pregnant, raises her hand.

ME: Yes, Loretta?

LORETTA: How old are you?

ME: I'd rather not say.

LORETTA: You married?

ME: No.

LORETTA: You got kids?

ME: Nope.

LORETTA: Why not?

ME: I just don't.

LORETTA: But you old.

ME: Not really.

LORETTA: That's just selfish right there.

ME Excuse me?

LORETTA: You ain't got no kids. That's selfish.

ME: That doesn't make any sense.

LORETTA: I bet your eggs is all dusty.

ME: That is just rude.

LORETTA: Man, you so selfish Miss.

Doris has spent the last two weeks on out-of-school suspension for pushing a teacher and telling

him to go fuck himself. It is her first day back at school.

ME: Welcome back Doris. How was your time off?

DORIS: It was awesome! My mom took me to get my nails done and we went shopping. I got these shoes and I got to sleep as late as I wanted.

ME: So you didn't get in trouble?

DORIS: No! My mom doesn't give a shit. She knows that teacher's an asshole.

ME: That's great that you have such a supportive mom.

ME: Everyone take out paper and pencils, we're having a quick reading quiz.

HERBIE: Hey Ms. Morris, what's that big red thing in the middle of your forehead?

ME: What do you think it is Herbie?

HERBIE: I don't know. That's why I asked.

ME: It's a pimple Herbie.

HERBIE: Oh.

ME: Yeah. Thanks for calling attention to it.

HERBIE: It ain't my fault. I didn't know. I thought it was like a big ass bug bite or sumthin. I was bouta' scratch that shit for you.

ME: How nice.

ME: This class is extremely out of control. This is why other teachers don't play games with you. Whenever I tell them I am going to play Jeopardy, they all say that they would never play a game like that!

FERN: Who cares about those other shitbag teachers!

ME: Maude, you've been late every day this week.

MAUDE: Why are you counting how many times I been late? You doin too much! Stop obsessing over me!

ME: Good morning everyone. I hope you had a nice weekend.

EDNA: You seem like you're in a good mood. Did you get laid?

ME: Today we will be talking about travel and the impact it has on us. Who would like to share a time when they had a memorable experience while traveling? Go ahead Ida.

IDA: When I was little I went with my parents to Hawaii. One night, I had a bad dream and went into my parents' room and I saw them having sex. It was disgusting.

ODYSSEUS IS A DOUCHE BAG

The following quotes are from actual student essays:

Choose a metaphor from Macbeth and explain the meaning behind it.

When Lady Macbeth says, "My hands are of your color; but I shame to wear a heart so white" she is really saying, "I am a two-faced terrible treacherous twat!"

In your opinion, is Odysseus worthy of the title hero?

Odysseus is not a hero, he's a douchebag.

In your opinion, is Odysseus worthy of the title hero?

Odysseus is my hero because he's the man. He's got a hot wife at home but then he goes around banging all these hoes around the globe. That's my dream right there.

Create an argument related to the sources on the assessment.

The essay question asks me to create an argument using sources from the assessment. How do I do that? An argument implies that there are two views or opinions which are being compared or contrasted. This would be impossible since every article on the assessment expresses the same opinion. But fear not, I have enough real life experience to make up for your bullshit question....

In closing, thanks for wasting an hour of my life reading about brain dead people with the combined intelligence of one orangutan.

Compare the tone or authors' attitudes in the two poems, "To Helen" by Edgar Allan Poe and "Helen" by HD.

The tones in the two poems about Helen of Troy are really different. One guy thinks she's totally the bait and the other guy thinks she's like the biggest ho.

Explain how Fitzgerald uses Nick Carraway to express the thematic element of conscience.

In The Great Gatsby by F. Scott Fitzgerald, the narrator Nick Carraway is used to express the theme of conscience. Fitzgerald uses Nick to contrast with the empty morals of East Eggers, such as Tom and Daisy. Fitzgerald stresses the importance of conscience to comment on the underlying ugliness of what many call the American dream. I should really continue writing about this topic, but to be honest, it is boring the crap out of me. I want to write about something else. And I know that most teachers only read the first paragraph of our essays, so I'm just going to fill in the rest with other stuff that is more fun. Like maybe I could write about cheese. I love all different kinds of cheese. American cheese is amazing as well as provolone. That's what makes pizza so much tastier, when they use provolone instead of mozzarella. What else should I talk about? How about how weird the people in this class are? Seriously, have you ever noticed the girl in the back with the dandruff? It's like all over her shoulders and it's really nasty. And the guy in the front row who is always squinting and clearing his throat so loudly and wiping his nose on his sleeve. It's like he's in 1st grade. Anyway, I guess this looks long enough and I'll end it. That is how Fitzgerald develops the theme of conscience in the context of the American dream.

Describe a notable experience or hardship you have endured and the lesson you learned.

In middle school I started experimenting with my sexuality. I had sex with this guy that was on my school bus. He told everyone at school that I'm fat and have a small dick. Everyone made fun of me. I had to switch schools. I hate him and I didn't really learn anything except that you can't trust other gay guys.

Describe a notable experience or hardship you have endured and the lesson you learned.

I cut myself all the time. I cut my arms and legs. I learned to wear long sleeves and pants so that no one can see the scars.

Write a letter to a Holocaust survivor of your choice. Express your feelings about their experience and ask any lingering questions you may have.

Dear Jew,

What's up? I was just reading about how you got shot in the neck but then pretended to be dead and crawled through the forest and stuff. When I read that I was like WHAAAT! That's gangsta! Anyways I got a few questions because my teacher wants me to ask you questions even tho you prolly dead by now. So remember when they rounded all you up and made you live in the getto and everything? Were you like so blown, just like wanting to kill them but you couldn't and everything? And also when they made you wear the yellow star, I was just wundrin why because like couldn't they tell you were Jews by looking at you? Why'd they have to make you wear that star? Anyways, don't get mad at God because he still loves you. I'm Catholic, so I know. You made it out that camp so that's how you know it's all good. It sucks how they killed your mom and sister and stuff. Life just be like that, happy then sad. Seriously tho, nice job with pretending to be dead and all. Air high five!

How does Hamlet's attitude toward revenge change throughout the play?

I don't know if Hamlet's attitude changes because I haven't been reading the play. I haven't been reading because I dislike Shakespeare or Sphere or however you spell that. It doesn't teach grammar and adds to my bad spelling because it's old English which is craptastically annoying. Even if you argue that craptastically isn't a word, which I'm sure you will, you get my point.

How was Winston and Julia's relationship an act of rebellion against the party in 1984?

Love is a bother. The very thought of it makes me want to puke. True love doesn't pay. You have to listen to them every day, buy stuff for them, and talk to them if they have problems. When it comes to gay marriage I do not approve but if they want to dig their own graves let them. This reminds me of a story. Long ago it was a warm Sunday morning I think the governor banned gay marriage and the gay people started a petition but he said no. They kept at it until he said yes. So marriage is about hard work and that's not for me. Love bores me and did you know that love backward is evil but change the o to an

i.

Write a one-page letter of introduction, including anything you would like me to know about you.

I am a student of many flaws and few redeeming qualities. I have a strong dislike for the subject of English and those who teach it. I would love to love literature but you make us read books that have little to no merit and tear apart students' papers and ridicule them with a slew of your red pen markings. This makes me despise the English subject. I would love to read a book that might teach me something about life and not some irrelevant bullshit. I would love to have a teacher who doesn't argue with me about my opinions and views. Sadly, I do not believe I will be blessed to have such an ideal class and competent teacher and therefore I cringe at my thoughts and predictions about this semester. There must be other things about me other than my complete hatred for the subject of English. I like to play World of Warcraft. I like math. I have a brother. I hope you help change my mind about English this semester.

Identify the strengths and weaknesses of the speaker's argument.

I seriously have no idea how to answer this so I'll just tell you about something I'm worried about. I don't want to just sit here and not write because then you'll ask me why I'm not writing anything. I think I may have gotten a girl pregnant. I don't even like her and she has a boyfriend already. So really I don't know if it's mine or not. I hope not.

Write an essay about the first chapter of the novel in which you explain how it foreshadows future events.

Since we're supposed to write about the first chapter I can't because I studied with Humphrey and Seymour yesterday and I went over the end of the book. I think Seymour did the beginning but he never told me about it so maybe you could look at his answer.

How is the text still relevant for today?

I really like it when you wear dresses. You should wear them more.

How do the various stereotypes about women presented in the text serve the author's purpose?

On the day we had that tornado drill is when we talked about this.

Describe how the author manages to give internal events the sense of excitement, suspense, and climax usually associated with external action.

This question is inappropriate and I'm not going to answer it.

Explain how the character's alienation reveals the surrounding society's assumptions or moral values.

This is a trick question and I will not be tricked!

Write a one-page letter of introduction, including anything you would like me to know about you.

Why are the people around me so open about their lives? Their grades, their activities, their thoughts are all pasted on a website for all the molesters and killers to see. 1984 warns of dependency on technology and how humanity is mutated rather than enlightened. I am different. I realize that the smiles and laughs around me are phony. I realize that the beauty most people see in each other is really a disgusting attempt for attention. I am better than them. I know the suffering that others read in books or watch on TV. I have experienced true love for my family and I have had it taken away from me. And I have survived. I will show them what true hatred is, true pain. I will push them away from me so that when they return, they will be stronger. I will save these people from their own destruction.

Name a book that changed your perspective on the world and describe how it impacted you.

A book that made the biggest impact on me is "Everyone Poops." It made me realize that pooping is nothing to be ashamed of. Everyone should read this book and realize that yes, everyone really does poop. That means it's okay, right? Right.

Name a book that changed your perspective on the world and describe how it impacted you.

A book that changed my perspective on the world is Fifty Shades of Grey. I loved it because it's like Twilight but more dirty and stuff. OMG! Christian Grey is so hot and Ana OMG! I couldn't put it down for a minute. It made me cry and I was a little worried at the end. But then I was like there's two more books so it's ok!

Name a book that changed your perspective on the world and describe how it impacted you.

I love Twilight it's so amazing how Edward saves Bella from the truck hitting her or when he sucks the venom from the bite from James. When he never leaves the hospital when she broke her leg and when they play baseball and James gang shows up and Edward gets defensive.

Name a book that changed your perspective on the world and describe how it impacted you.

I hate reading it bores me and I HATE big books so I saw Twilight and said to myself another book about vampires this is going to suck and I really didn't want to read it because it was so big but since nothing else interested me and everyone was like omg you have to read this book I bought it and I found out that I had finished a 500 page book in less then two days and I was so happy cause I never read a big book like that but anyways there isn't anyone in the world who don't wish Edward Cullen was real cause I do seriously and it made me think maybe vampires really do exist.

Name a book that changed your perspective on the world and describe how it impacted you.

I'd pick Thug-a-licious because there's so much drama and twists and turns and shit you don't expect.

College application essay question: Evaluate a significant experience you have had and its impact on you.

A significant experience I had was my second abortion.

Respond to the following quote, "To be creative one must be a touch insane."

Humans are not Vulcans. But autistic people are. Most humans see autistics as weird and crazy but really they are Vulcan.

Write a memoir using only six words.

Want love, only got deez hoes.

Write a memoir using only six words.

I'm smiling but dreaming of murder.

In order for me to get to know you better, please complete the following sentence: If you really knew me, you'd know that…

If you really knew me you'd know that I'm a pothead.

What is at the top of your "bucket list" (things you want to do before you die)?

I wanna go to Jamaica to smoke that good shit.

Write a one-page reflection on the activity we did in class today.

In order to reflect on today's activity, a strong skill of talking BS is required, which I don't have.

Using a similar tone and style to that of the author of "How to Spot a Witch," write an article entitled, "How to Spot a _____," and fill in the blank with a type of person for whom you can write a detailed description.

MILF is an acronym that stands for "mother I'd like to f-ck." MILFs are women who are still attractive, even if they're more than 30 and have had several children. In the erotic dreams of teenagers, MILFs are highly sought. So how do you spot one?

-Awesome Body and Beautiful Tits: According to many online guides, the first thing about a MILF that catches one's eye is her hot body. If the woman is 30-35 years old, tall and athletic with nice breasts and long hair, she's probably a MILF. Here is a simple test: just take the suspected woman in front of a dozen heterosexual teenagers and if their jaws drop and their eyes are wide open, then she's a MILF.

- The Lingerie Store: Usually a MILF is dissatisfied with her husband or is divorced and she tries to look hot to capture the attention of young good looking boys. Compelling evidence is the underwear she wears. If she buys provocative garter belts, thongs, and lacy bras in a lingerie store then there is no doubt that she's a MILF.

-The Diet: A MILF must avoid sweets, fats and carbohydrates to remain attractive. Bring her to a fast food restaurant and if she orders a diet coke and a salad and talks about dieting she might be a MILF.

WARNING: Once a MILF seduces you, there is no way out. Any attempt to speak of age differences or the law is useless and may even increase her attraction to you!

Write a fully developed essay in which you argue for or against the summer reading policy.

ESSAY
I don't Know I really don't care

YOU ARE WHAT YOU WEAR

Here is a list of quotes from t-shirts that students have worn to my class:

Ben Dover

Bust a Nut (that's what she said)

Oh shit!

Boobs Vagina Tits Vagina

I direct midget porn

Fuck you you fucking fuck

My other ride is your mom

Fart loading… please wait

I am sofa king wee todd did

To do list: You, your friend, your sister, your mom

I like big boobs and I cannot lie

Five dollar foot long (with a big arrow pointing downwards)

Don't be sexist, bitches hate that

Got boobs?

(If you don't recognize this one, I suggest you Google "the shocker")

LET'S SMOKE SOME METH

In my school, teachers have to watch every single thing that comes out of their mouths because the students created a website dedicated solely to quoting teachers who say inappropriate things. While a teacher is supposed to know what should and should not be said in front of a class of teenagers, many quotes are much worse when taken out of context.

For example, the quote, "Let's talk about breasts," might sound pretty inappropriate if the fact that it was Breast Cancer Awareness Day was not included. Also, hearing that a teacher said, "Let's smoke some meth" might strike someone as extremely inappropriate. But the context of the quote is vital. He or she merely asked the class what rhymes with *Macbeth*, and when a student answered "meth" he placed the word into the play to show how silly it was. "Let's go smoke some meth, and with his former title greet Macbeth?" Everyone laughed and the class moved on with the lesson.

Another example is when I told a student that she is a ho. Out of context, this would sound pretty terrible; therefore it is imperative that you know the situation in which it occurred. The class was reading *The Crucible*, and a student got confused about the part she was playing. While she was in the middle of playing Abigail, John Proctor's mistress, she stopped to ask why she would act a certain way if she was his wife. To clarify, I reminded her that Abigail is his

79

mistress. She said, "So I'm a ho?" To which I replied, "Yes, you are a ho. If that is how you choose to word it." See? Not so bad. But remove this fact from the circumstance and it looks pretty awful.

It probably looks rather horrible when you read that I told a student I was going to send him back to Africa. But the quote does not include the background information about the student telling me that if he ever got in trouble in school his parents told him they would send him back to Africa. Thus, we had an on-going joke when he misbehaved about my calling home and his resulting trip to Africa. It eventually broke down to my joking about where he would end up. But without the explanation, I'm sure I look pretty racist and terrible.

It's all about context, and students love to remove it.

THE TIPPING POINT

After we finish reading a novel, I like to give a creative homework assignment that asks students to design a visual representation of their favorite scene. This is a very easy task. All they must do is choose an illustration (either one they make themselves or something taken from the internet), and write a synopsis of the scene, including a quote from the text. With minimal effort, the assignment might take five minutes.

Despite the simplicity of the assignment, there is always someone who forgets to do it and quickly scrawls a shitty stick figure onto a piece of paper. I am insulted when they try to hand it in, and I immediately reject it. On this particular day, that is what Dorothy did. I looked at her with contempt and said, "You must be out of your mind." She took her paper back and it ended up on the floor underneath her desk.

During the next class, Igor had also forgotten his homework. He found Dorothy's stick figure under his desk, which now had a huge, dirty footprint on it and quickly scribbled the title of the book across the top. When he put the paper out in front of me, I thought I was dreaming. "You must be joking," I said. He shrugged his shoulders. "You're actually trying to hand this in?"

He shrugged his shoulders again. "You found this on the floor!" I yelled.

81

"Gimme a break!" With anger, Igor swiped his paper from my hand, crumpled it up and shoved it into his desk.

The next class came in and I saw that Herman, who generally hands his work in on time, was particularly upset because he had forgotten to do the assignment. A few minutes later I almost fell over when I saw the crumpled up piece of paper with the same stick figure and footprint in Herman's hand. He had added his name to the back of the paper. I lost it.

"How stupid do you think I am?" I said. Herman completely froze.

"I mean, don't you have any dignity?" I cried out. "Two other students just tried to hand in the same garbage you just found on the floor!" Herman was silent and so was the class. "What would you do if you were me?" I asked. "Huh? If you were me, and I tried to hand in the crumpled up stick figure with a dirty footprint on it, what would you do?" Herman said nothing. "Tell me Herman! Am I supposed to accept this work? Am I?" Again, nothing from Herman, who was slowly losing the color from his face. I admit, I was going way overboard with this, but he had become the tipping point.

"Okay," I declared, "You be me and I'll be you!" Herman looked like he was going to cry. "Hey teacher!" I said in a mocking tone. "Here's this dirty piece of paper I just found on the floor. It's my homework!" I held the paper out to Herman, who did not respond. "Now tell me what I'm supposed to do, teacher! Tell me! You be me! How are you going to respond?" Thankfully, Herman remained silent, and I spun around and quickly jumped into the day's lesson. I completely overreacted, and with a more obnoxious student, that exchange could have ended very badly. But sometimes, there is only so much a teacher can take!

VALENTINE'S DAY SURPRISE

On Valentine's Day, the following drawing was left in my mailbox:

It was drawn on the inside of a ripped up conversation hearts box.

A WILDLIFE HABITAT CALLED MIDDLE SCHOOL

Before I started teaching full time in high school, I had a brief leave replacement in a middle school. Human beings age 12 to 14 are like a separate species from the rest of the population. They act, think and even smell differently from the rest of us. Thankfully, most of them find some sense of civilization around the time they enter high school. But during those strange years when they are no longer children, but definitely not adults, they adopt very unusual behaviors and habits.

One of the major issues with middle schoolers these days is that they have the bodies of forty-year-olds with the minds of elementary school kids. Many sixth-grade males have full grown mustaches and deep manly voices. The females often develop more fully than their own mothers. This shit is highly confusing. They look like adults but act like cave dwellers. And for most of them, their biggest challenge is conquering personal hygiene.

Take Shirley for example. Although only a 7th grader, Shirley had humongous breasts the size of soccer balls. If she weren't twelve, I would assume they were implants. She wore bras that were way too small and very low cut shirts and as another teacher put it, she would "squeeze her two Christmas hams" into a low-cut V-neck, most often times with words like SEXY or HOT printed on the front. She kept everything in between her breasts, which was awkwardly clever. If you caught her using a cell phone she would wedge it into her cleavage, just daring you to ask her to remove it. It was super festive when she would receive a call and her chest would light up and play music. She also kept several pens, pencils, erasers, tissues, lip glosses and her homework crammed in there. On my last day she pulled me into an awkwardly tight embrace and whispered into my ear, "They're real."

Fred was another remarkable junior high creature. Fred was extremely overweight, wore very tight t-shirts, and either he sweated specifically from his nipples or had the ability to lactate. He also ate erasers, pencils, paper, tape and pen caps. On one occasion, he ate most of a pen until it exploded in his mouth and was running down his chin and neck. He didn't realize at first and continued chewing away gleefully, looking like a psychotic cartoon monster. Fred also had significant foot fungus issues. It was a constant fight to get him to keep his shoes on because he said his feet were "really friggin' itchy" and he couldn't really scratch them without completely exposing them. When he removed his shoes, it was like someone had introduced an airborne toxin into the classroom atmosphere, and everyone would protest. One day a student came up to me with tears in her eyes and said, "You have to move my seat. I have to be as far away from him as possible. It burns my eyes!" For this reason, I insisted that Fred sit by an open window at all times, regardless of the weather conditions.

Besides his foot odor and lactation, Fred sang old sea shanties during exams and had the fascinating/revolting habit of picking his nose and saving his findings in a Ziploc bag. He would often take out the bag and remove some of its contents to snack on. I'll take a moment to let you wipe that image from your mind.

Clarence was rather small for his age, but his personality certainly packed a punch. He showed up twenty minutes late for our first class. When I asked where he had been, he replied, "None of yo' b'niss beeotch!" I was awe-struck by his forthrightness. I asked him to sit in the empty desk at the back of the room and he replied, "You mean the one with the dick on it?" He was right; the desk did have an enormous penis drawn on it. "That's right," I replied.

For three classes, I was greeted with a "Sup Beeotch!" or a "Damn, you one ugly muthafucka!" I wrote him up for verbal abuse and inappropriate behavior, but to no avail. During our fourth class together we went to the computer lab.

Clarence spent the entire class translating the word penis from English to various foreign languages such as Japanese, turning up the speakers on the computer, and repeatedly hitting the translate button. He was finally removed and placed into a class entitled, "Appropriateness in Social Situations," or ASS Class for short. I hope he did well there.

My most challenging middle school specimen was Estelle. On my first day, she gave me a handwritten list of her self-diagnosed mental illnesses. The list included the following:

1) Sometimes I get bi-polar and shit.

2) I get real mad.

3) Don't talk to me if I wear red. Red is my angry color and it means I'm going threw something.

4) I haven't choked nobody since 2nd grade.

5) I pick the color blue for you but don't ever wear red cuz it's mine.

At first I was constantly writing referrals for Estelle refusing to sit anywhere but behind my desk, hitting students in the back of the neck with various classroom objects, and threatening to "bust" on anyone who spoke to her. At least once a week, I would catch her writing ransom notes to her history teacher. She told me she stole at least one thing from his room each week and then gave him five chances to get it back. She said that five chances are better than three because, "Three is just racist."

When I asked the class to list their strengths as writers, she wrote, "Cash, money, hoes."

After many months of pleading with Estelle to find a seat of her own, she finally agreed. But then a special education teacher started attending class to work with certain students. Estelle sat behind my desk again that day, and would not return to her seat. Because she was wearing red at the time, I approached carefully and sat down next to her.

"What's up?" I asked. "That bitch is weird," she said. "Which one?" I asked. "The lady who's all up in here all the time. What she got to be in here for? Did you tell her about my bi-polars?" she asked.

"No. Your bi-polars are private business. And by the way, I meant to thank you for that list. I found it very informative. I admire your candor. You're a courageous young woman," I said.

"I don't know what the fuck you're talking about but thanks," she responded.

After that, I became Estelle's personal therapist. She visited me daily, after school, to tell me about what had stressed her out that day. I decided to give her a "Daily Stress Journal" which consisted of a chart that asks the student to list the details of what causes them tension. Her chart described the following situations:

1. Drama

2. You think your better then me?

3. Teachers

4. Told the bus driver to shut up

I asked Estelle to explain why she told the bus driver to shut up. She said, "I was late for the bus and I had to run to catch it cuz the bitch wouldn't stop. When she stopped I got in and had to sit next to this retard cuz there weren't any seats. I threw my bagel at the back window and it stuck there. Everyone was laughing, but it wasn't my fault. I didn't think it would stick. Then the driver told me to clean up my mess and that's when I told her to shut the fuck up. But I said please."

Estelle was given a lunch detention for her episode with the bus driver. However, she felt her lunch detention should be excused because it was Black History Month and she should get a free pass, at least until March. She wrote a letter to the principal and asked me to pass it along just in case he didn't take her argument seriously. The letter read, "**It is against my rights to serve detention because I didt do anything wrong and you are all retards and the 14 amenmet clearly states that slavery is over so I don't have to do anything I don't want to and cuz you aint my daddy nor are you my mom and I aint a slave. So you can't tell me what to do cuz its civil rights!**" You have to admire Estelle for her strength of character and resolve.

Of all the middle school creatures I encountered, Lance was the most fascinating. On my first day, he ran around the room in circles refusing to sit down. Then he hit another kid straight in the center of his back with a giant yardstick. Next, he took off his shirt and pressed his bare breast against a female student's face. He joyfully asked her if she liked the way his nipples smelled. This was quite fun to type into the school's referral system. Lance also wrote love poems for me on a weekly basis. The best one said, "You are like a rose growing in sand, Can't you tell me why I can't be your man?" Each week I would find a new poem in my school mailbox along with a half-eaten snack. I asked the secretary if she had seen him drop them off. She said she didn't even think he actually went to our school. That was comforting.

Lance was creepy. I was genuinely afraid of him. He once offered to bring in chloroform for a class party. While the other kids wrote things like, "Cheetos" and "soda" on the sign-up sheet, Lance wrote, "Chips, Chlorophorm." I didn't question him, ever.

There is something about study hall that really brought out the worst in my middle school students. Maybe it was because there was no lesson plan or set activity. It was a time set aside for homework and studying and it was completely self-motivated. I was essentially a babysitter for that block of time. When you ask a twelve-year-old boy to entertain himself for an hour, you are asking for trouble. One student actually stapled a piece of paper to his forehead. It was the most horrific thing I have ever seen. Another student flung open a window and started throwing kids' backpacks and books out into the street. I was careful not to provoke him when I threw him out because he had just been removed from a different study hall for punching his pregnant teacher in the stomach. His only punishment for that was just being removed from that study hall and placed into mine.

Amongst the chaos of study hall I couldn't help but notice a group of girls working feverishly on a chart. This chart turned out to be the most disturbing thing I learned about middle school life: they charted their sexual experiences and determined each other's level of coolness and acceptance based upon these ratings. Each sexual act got a point value; the more scandalous the act, the higher the point value. Points were also added for location and number of partners. For example, a girl had sex with two boys in the boys' bathroom. This earned her ten points for the sex, an extra two points for the additional partner and an added five points for the dangerous location. She also received another five points because one of those boys was considered the most popular boy in the school. For the total amount of points, she received the honor of wearing a hot pink wristband, which served as a symbol to the other students of her sexual status and popularity. The school eventually found out about the chart and prohibited the wristbands. They also suspended the girl who had sex in the bathroom, though her parents could not understand why. They felt that the punishment was way too harsh for their daughter and fought it pretty hard. Perhaps they should have cared more about the fact that their 13-year-old daughter was having a threesome at school? (Just saying...)

BRAIN DAMAGE

According to the National Institute of Mental Health, being a teenager is extremely hazardous to one's health. "Mortality rates jump between early and late adolescence. Rates of death by injury between ages 15 to 19 are about six times that of the rate between ages 10 and 14. Crime rates are highest among young males."[15] MRI comparisons between teenage brains and the brains of adults have shown that most of the areas are the same except for the immaturity of the adolescent brain in the frontal lobe, the area that controls impulses and decision-making. Apparently teenagers rely on their "more primitive limbic system" in interpreting and reacting to emotion since they lack the more "mature cortex that can override the limbic response."[16]

I once saw an exhibit about brains at a science museum. It claimed that when scientists studied the brains of teenagers, the decision-making areas of their brains closely resembled that of an adult with brain damage. The following incidents will prove this finding to be decidedly true:

• A student decided it would be "fun" to throw a five-pound textbook from the third-floor railing at school. It hit a girl on the head resulting in a brief coma and ironically, permanent brain damage.

• One student defecated on the stage in the auditorium, one in the stacks of the school library, and another on the staircase during school hours. This was

90

confirmed through security camera footage. Students often shit in the bathroom sink (or shit somewhere else and move it to the sink). One student shit in a bag and left it in classroom.

• A student stole one book each week from the school library and smeared feces on the pages before returning them. He was caught through his public tweets about it.

• A group of male students created a game called "Rappelling" where they would jump off the roof of a three-story house to see whose injuries would be the most severe. The kid who needed his head stapled back together won.

• Another group of male students decided to run through a crowded mall completely naked. One got arrested.

• The same group of students pooled all of their pocket change, bought hundreds of tacos and burritos at Taco Bell, and put them into the pockets of various garments at expensive department stores.

• Several groups of male students were caught punching each other in the testicles with great force during lunch. They claimed they were playing a game called "Sack Tapping."

• "Forking" is a new trend among local teens. It involves sticking thousands of forks into the front lawn of an enemy's house. My school was "forked." Cleaning up after this was not a great use of the custodians' time.

• A teacher who is hated by many students had her house "forked," but attached to the forks were maxi pads with tomato sauce poured on them.

• For their senior prank, a group of students decided to spray-paint all of the classroom doors in different neon colors. They did this directly in front of security cameras while wearing their senior class sweatshirts with their last names written on them.

• A few years ago, students at my school thought it would be funny to drop LSD into the water bottle of their teacher. He began hallucinating in front of them and had to be hospitalized. It wasn't funny.*

*Okay, it was a little funny.

FROM THE FRONTLINES

Part I

I asked a group of elementary, middle and high school teachers to describe the most challenging, absurd or outrageous incident they have had in the classroom. This is what I received:

"I was purposely tripped and pushed to the ground when I was six months pregnant."

"A major drug ring was busted in my class. They found 3 lbs. of hash."

"My student entered the class covered in blood and calmly sat down after trying to kill someone outside my door."

"When my back was turned a student slammed his head extremely hard onto a desk because he wanted to quell the voices in his head."

"The time a middle schooler was fighting, had his teeth knocked out, grabbed them out of his mouth and threw them, hitting the counselor in the head, and kept fighting."

"Two boys in kindergarten pulled out their private parts and showed the class what they were working with."

"A kid pulled out a molar with his bare hands."

"Some kindergarteners play with themselves during naptime."

"On my first day of class at a new school, a student took off all his clothes, peed, and sprawled out on the floor, refusing to get up."

"During a fight between an 8th-grade girl and a 7th-grade boy, a co-worker tried to restrain the boy. The kid bit the teacher's nipple through his shirt and he had to get stitches."

"A kid dropped trou, laid cable in the hall and then stepped in it, tracking it all the way down the hallway."

"I had to stop one kindergartener from shoving a frosted mini wheat up another student's ass."

"A 5th grader was playing with her feces in the bathroom and fell asleep in it."

"7th-grade boys tried to gouge each other's eyes out."

"3rd graders bitch slapping each other."

"I had a student store poop in his desk."

"One of my kindergarteners stabbed another student with a pair of safety scissors that went right through his hand."

"I had a student cut his legs while yelling that he was a vampire. Then he licked his blood and hissed at us."

"In the middle of literature class, kids lit up a joint and began passing it."

"A massive fight broke out because a girl blocked the TV for a second. One of the girls ended up topless and refused to put her shirt back on."

"During a massive tantrum, a 3rd grader threw a chair at my head and I had to get stitches."

REALLY REAL EMAILZ: STUDENT EDITION

From: Pablo the student

To: English Teacher

Subject: Test Today

Hi, the world cup is on tv today the same time as the final. Can I be excused so I can watch it? I really really really want to watch it!

From Pablo

From: Vern the student

To: English Teacher

Subject: My Grade

I'm going to be honest here, I'm extremely disappointed with my grade that I got on the final exam especially because this test is worth so many points, and it is going to effect my grade drastically. I studied really hard for this so I was not expecting this. I've worked really hard at this class, and feel like I personally deserve the A that I earned in this class, because of all the hours and effort I put in and this one test is going to bring my whole grade down, along with my GPA. So if the test brings down my overall grade is there anything I can do to bring up my grade, like anything? My grade is really upsetting me and I know that it isn't my fault if I didn't do well because I studied and did the work so maybe the teaching wasn't that good. But please let me know if there is anything I can do.

Thanks,

Vern

From: Mildred the student

To: English Teacher

Subject: My Grade

Dear Ms. Morris,

I know you said that you would return our projects on Monday, but I need to know what my grade is now because if my project didn't pass, that would mean I'd have three failing grades already, and then I don't think I have a great chance of passing your class, so I wouldn't need to do the paper that is due on Wednesday.

So before Monday's class could you let me know if I passed the project so I know if I should do the paper? And if I didn't, could you explain why and if there's any way I can still pass your class?

I don't want to hear the bad news in class so please don't wait, just email me. If I did as well as I hoped I did, then I can know ahead of time and get to school on time.

Thanks,

Mildred

From: Wanda, a former student

To: English Teacher

Subject: Wassup

Hey Ms. Morris, wanna chill? Can I getcha digits?

From: Franz the student

To: English Teacher

Subject: Email address

Hi Ms. Morris. I was just wondering if I could have your email address so I can send you my paper. Thanks! Franz

(NOTE: Yes, this question was sent in an EMAIL.)

From: Wanda, your former student

To: English Teacher

Subject: Wassup

Wassup wit dat, Imma talk from da hood now. I email u and asked wassup and u never reply. Come on now dawg. Anyways do u have like another email and can I gettcha numbah plzzzzz and oh yea btw dun make me bring my ass up there and cut u up. JK. Imma tell you sumthing if you reply sumthing.

From: Archibald the student

To: English Teacher

Subject: Sorry

Dear Miss Morris,

They said I have to write you a letter of apology so I want to begin first by apologizing for disrespecting you. I know that it was rude of me. I should have never called you a "sexy thang." I realize that this term is used as sexual harastment towards women. You are my teacher so I should respect you and everything. I'm sorry.

(NOTE: This was a "punishment.")

From: Boris the student

To: English Teacher

Subject: My grade

Umm so I know that I haven't been coming to class and when I do I pretty much sleep the whole time but there is only a week left of school and I have a 23% and if I don't pass I won't graduate so can you please give me make up work. If you don't I won't graduate.

From: Thelma, someone else's student

To: English Teacher

Subject: Second Opinion

Dear Ms. Morris,

I am a student in Mrs. Wagonwheeler's 12th grade English class. My friend has you for the same class and I know you did the same paper as us. Mrs. Wagonwheeler gave me a bad grade on the paper and I worked very hard on it, and feel I do not deserve the grade I got. I've asked her if I can redo it but she keeps saying no. I would really appreciate it if you could also grade the paper because it makes up a big portion of my grade in the class. I put a copy of the paper in your mailbox, and I also attached it to this email. If you could email me back what grade you think I should get I would really appreciate it.

Thank you,

Thelma

From: Roy the student

To: English Teacher

Subject: Donation

Hi Miss, I'm asking my teachers to donate money for the signup fee for summer school. My mom don't have enough money. If you want to leave it in your mailbox and I can pick it up later. Thank you!

(NOTE: Roy has only attended class twice the entire semester. This email was sent on the last day to register for summer school.)

From: Virgil the student

To: English Teacher

Subject: Protest

I am writing to protest the due date of the reading questions for next class. Considering this is one of the longest sections in the book, the speed seems excessive. In my personal life I have other things to do, and the Scarlet Letter is to me so dense and boring that it easily takes me an hour to read 20 pages; 40 pages would therefore take around two. I have other homework to do as well, and a personal life I'd like to maintain, and given time restraints I have prioritized all of these above your reading questions. I would not be as infuriated by this timing if you accepted late work, especially since this is homework. Finally, the reading questions themselves are ridiculous. You could say they shouldn't take much time, as there are only seven of them, but given that you seem to expect long answers for each one, the amount of work is frankly ludicrous. I will not be completing this assignment on time, and do to the reasons listed above, I expect you to accept my work late.

Virgil

From: Liesel the student

To: English Teacher

Subject: Comments on my papers

Dear Ms. Morris,

When giving feedback on my papers, I'd appreciate it if you would not put things in bold or use capital letters. It feels to me as if you are yelling at me, which I do not appreciate. I am trying my best to meet your requirements and I would greatly appreciate it if you could try to meet mine too.

Liesel

From: Thaddeus the student

To: English Teacher

Subject: tests i missed

Yo Miss Morris, i no i missed those other 2 tests from the begin of the yr so just count this one we bout to take 3 times (I wouldn't want to give u extra grading anywy)

Thnx Tad

From: Sigmund the Student

To: English Teacher

Subject: Beach Week!

Hey so like next week is beach week and I really wanna go so can I take the final early?

From: Brunhilda the Student

To: English Teacher

Subject: oops!

I brought you my college essay to edit yesterday and

I know you said that you'd have it next week but I just realized that it's actually due today and you have the only copy b/c I didn't save it! Can you type it up for me with your edits and email it to me as soon as you can? I need it today!

Thanks!

From: Yurgin the student

To: English Teacher

Subject: Form!

Ms. Morris! I checked with my counselor this morning and she said she didn't get the recommendation form I gave you yesterday! It is due today and I need it to get my transcript! Do the form TODAY!

Yurgin

II.PARENTS

"Teaching is not a lost art, but the regard for it is a lost tradition."

Jacques Barz

THE CRAZY APPLE DOESN'T FALL FAR FROM THE CRAZY TREE

Earl was smart but lazy. He decided he hated me and my class after I gave an assignment that he refused to complete because it "violated his right to privacy." The assignment was a research paper that every 12th grade student was required to complete. They were also required to hand in their paper through an internet-based plagiarism-detection service. The service merely asks the student to submit their paper, privately, and it checks their sources to make sure they are accurate. The reason the school began using this program is obviously because too many kids were cutting and pasting whole parts of their papers from the internet. They also copy from each other. I explained this to Earl. He fought me with an intense anger in class. He accused me of not trusting him. I said that I trust all of my students, but I was merely following school policy. He said I was "misguided." I told him to speak to the head of the English department for any further grievances. The next morning, the department chair received the following letter on her desk:

To Whom It May Concern,

My name is Earl and I am currently a student in Ms. Morris' third period class. Today, I am inquiring over the current policy that requires all students to use turnitin.com for their senior research paper. According to Ms. Morris, it is a fact that this is the policy for the entire English department. If this is so, I request my exemption from the use of turnitin.com or any other plagiarism recognition software due to my beliefs regarding cheating, human communication, technology and privacy.

A lot of people cheat. This is a cold, hard fact that many people have come to accept. While I do not condone cheating, I submit that education's solution to cheating is to assume that everyone cheats. Thus, educational "tools" such as turnitin.com are used to patrol the already guilty students. Not only is this wrong upon many moral and ethical levels, but it fails to recognize the student as an equal and contributes to the breakdown of communication between students, teachers and administrators.

In our public schools, the aforementioned breakdown is a result of overzealous PTA members and bureaucratic administrators. Due to these inconveniences, teaching is no longer the undisputed priority of teachers. Now they are encompassed with menial tasks and ever expanding red tape beset by the image-focused administration. Instead of teaching, teachers spend their time filling out detrimental paperwork and are forced to spread the administration's propaganda. Due to their limited time, simple yet important things like checking the sources of a student's research paper are cut down and turned over to third parties like turnitin.com. Suffice to say, the mistrust of students has led to the technological implementations that oversee students, like this website, automated absentee messages, loss of credit notifications, online access to grade books and more.

In the 21st century, it is close to impossible to live in this country without the use of modern technology. While I am not a Luddite, I contend that technology has led to the breakdown of communication and social interaction. No longer do we talk face to face, but send text messages and emails. Upon this reason of thought, I cannot submit to the mechanical and robotic perils of turnitin.com.

Most importantly, this software entails the violation of privacy guaranteed to every United States citizen. Due to their wide database, strangers may be given access to my work. Simply put, I do not want John Doe from Anytown, U.S.A. reading a paper I wrote for my high school English class.

No one can deny that cheating is a prevalent issue in our society. While this may be the case, we cannot forget the exceeding importance of human communication, and the right to privacy. The use of turnitin.com reinforces the misguided belief that students are not to be trusted. Nonetheless, I am asking you to exempt me from the use of this program and I also ask that you consider removing the policy completely.

Sincerely,

Earl

While some of what Earl said had merit, and I appreciated him taking a stand for overworked teachers everywhere, a lot of what he wrote was downright ridiculous. Regardless of how we felt about his argument, my boss decided to call his bluff. She called him into her office, along with me, and said that she read his letter and understood and respected his point of view. However, in lieu of the plagiarism detection site, Earl would need to print and photocopy every one of his sources, highlight each quote and create corresponding numbers for his bibliography instead. While this would require a substantial amount of work, compared to the ease of the website, she would have no problem with it, since it would not infringe on his right to privacy. After about ten seconds of silence Earl replied, "Fuck that. I'll just use the site," and with that he got up and left her office. For a young man with such conviction, he dropped his cause pretty quickly when faced with a little extra work.

A few days later I gave my classes their first journal assignment. Being a rookie teacher, I didn't know about the creative/personal writing disclaimer that all teachers know to give. I only wanted to give my students a way to express themselves without being bogged down by harsh requirements. So I said, "The only requirement for journal entries is length and effort. The content is completely up to you. While I will give you a topic to start with, you may go in any direction you choose. Use stream of consciousness and don't worry about spelling or grammar. Use your journal as a way to explore your mind." (I now know that this must be promptly followed by this disclaimer: While I encourage you to be open and honest, I am still your teacher, and your journals must remain school appropriate. If you write anything alarming, such as wanting to hurt yourself or someone else, I have a legal responsibility to contact your counselor and the school administration. If you write anything that is blatantly inappropriate, I will have to take disciplinary action.)

I should have realized there was going to be a problem when Earl raised his hand and asked, "So we can write about anything we want?" I was naïve and answered, "Yes." The journal prompt I gave was, "What is your heaviest burden right now?" since we were reading *The Things They Carried*, a novel about young soldiers in the Vietnam War. Earl stayed after class a few minutes to finish his four-page long journal entry. He brought it up to my desk and held it out in front of me. When I went to take it, he pulled it back and said, "So you won't show this to anyone else, right?" I thought he wrote something emotional about his family life that he wouldn't want me to bring up in front of the class. "Right," I replied. "You're the only one that is going to read this?" he asked again. "Yup, I won't show it to anyone." It didn't occur to me that he was asking these questions precisely because he knew he wrote something entirely inappropriate and didn't want to get into trouble. I thought he needed someone to open up to and was reaching out. Boy did he teach me a lesson. He handed me the paper and walked out. Of course, I immediately read it and knew I had a huge problem on my hands. Apparently Earl's heaviest burden was the result of his overly active sex life. Here is merely an excerpt from his unbelievably disgusting journal entry:

"My heaviest burden is women, the ones I have sex with in particular. After you sleep with a girl, she becomes unbearably attached. It's pathetic. I get phone calls and texts constantly from girls I no longer have a sexual interest in. Once I have experienced them in that way, I feel I have no use for them. But they become extremely clingy, as though what we did was the equivalent of some kind of emotional contract and not merely an activity to pass time. Take this girl Florence Burger for example. We talked in the hallway for a while, and I convinced her to let me come to her house one night. I climbed into her window and talked her into having sex with me. The sex was mediocre and I was rather bored. When it was over she started crying. She revealed that she was a virgin. After that, I felt obligated to stay there and talk with her. I made her feel better, but she became attached right away. Now she calls me every day and I find her attachment to me extremely unattractive. Why don't girls understand that once I've had sex with them it is almost impossible to maintain interest? I refuse to believe that my own psychology is at the source of this problem."

Since I told Earl specifically that I wasn't going to share his journal with anyone, I only explained the gist of it to my department head. She told me to use it as a "teaching moment," by lecturing Earl about morals and how to respect women. I told her I wasn't comfortable with that. She said the alternative would be to call his parents. I said I felt weird about it because I reiterated to Earl that I would not share his journal with anyone. She said that I would not have to explicitly share the contents of the journal, but merely explain that it was inappropriate. That sounded like a viable option. So I took a deep breath and dialed Earl's home number. His mother answered.

"Hello, this is Ms. Morris, Earl's English teacher. I'm calling to inform you of an incident that occurred in class today."

"Okay," the mother said with a hint of attitude.

"I gave the students a creative writing assignment. They were supposed to write about their heaviest burden. Earl's writing was very inappropriate."

"Well, what did it say?" his mother asked.

"The thing is that I told the students what they wrote would remain private. But I can tell you that it was extremely inappropriate and of a sexual nature."

"Well, if you aren't going to tell me exactly what it said, then how do you expect me to speak to him about it?"

"Maybe you can just have a conversation with him about school appropriateness," I said.

"Well, how can I do that if I don't know what it said?" she replied, with a very nasty tone.

"I don't even feel comfortable reading this thing aloud. That is how inappropriate it is."

"So fax it to me."

"I just really don't feel comfortable sharing his work since I told him it would remain private."

"If you told him it would remain private, why are you telling me about it?"

"I did not realize how inappropriate the contents would be."

"Perhaps the assignment was inappropriate. What was the assignment?"

"The assignment was to write an open-ended journal about the student's heaviest burden. It relates to themes in the book we are reading."

"Well, if you aren't going to tell me exactly what he wrote then there is nothing I can do."

"Okay. Well…"

"Ms. Morris, how many years have you been teaching?"

"This is my first year."

"That's obvious. Look, I have my doctorate in educational theory and I think I can help you. I'm going to email you several essays. May I have your email address?"

"Sure."

"Great. I look forward to your response. Goodbye."

I never received any emails from Earl's mom and forgot all about it. A few weeks later I received the following phone call in the office:

"Hello, this is Ms. Morris…"

"Why didn't you answer my emails?"

"I'm sorry, who is this?"

"This is Earl's mom! I sent you several emails and asked you to reply that you got them and I never received anything from you. I even spoke to my son about his journal and I asked you to follow up!"

"I'm so sorry, but I never got any emails from you."

"You are full of shit!"

As she continued to scream into the phone, I said, "You cannot speak to me that way. I am hanging up now."

After I had hung up the phone, it rang again. Another teacher answered it and said that I wasn't available. She hung up and called again until she got the office answering machine. She said that if I didn't pick up the phone and talk to her she would come to the school to speak with me in person. I ignored it. Twenty minutes later she arrived at the main office, demanding to talk to me.

The Ass. Principal asked me to come to her office to meet with Earl's mom. When I entered the room, it was full of other administrators who were trying to calm her down. When she saw me, she stood up, pointed at me, and screamed, "This is the most unprofessional teacher I have ever encountered! She never answered my emails and hung up on me!" The Ass. Principal asked her to sit down, but she refused. I said that I had never received any emails. She said I was a liar. I said that I only hung up on her because she was cursing at me. Again, she said I was a liar. The Ass. Principal asked how they could resolve the situation. She demanded that I be fired. Thankfully, they stood up for me and said that even if her claims were true, it would not be grounds for dismissal. She screamed, "This is bullshit!" and swung open the door to the office, then slammed it shut.

We all sat in silence for a few seconds. Then the Ass. Principal said, "Ms. Morris. You never hang up on a parent." I couldn't believe what I was hearing and replied, "But she was cursing at me!" She took a deep breath and replied, "I know. But you *never* hang up on a parent." I just said, "Okay," and before long the meeting was dismissed.

Earl came in the next day with copies of his mother's emails to me. She had spelled my email address wrong. I asked him to tell her this. I never heard from her again.

NO SEX ON THE STAIRCASE

My school is huge. It has several floors with numerous corridors and winding hallways. In between classes, the halls are filled wall to wall with bodies. During class, many of the corridors are empty. It was during a walk down a hallway I had never been through that I decided to take a remote staircase I had never been on. Big mistake.

As I started down the staircase, I could barely believe what stood before me. There in the middle of the stairs were two students, completely butt naked except for their socks, having sex from behind. If I would have had a moment to think, I would probably have run back up the stairs and pretended that I hadn't seen anything. But my natural reaction was to scream and throw all of my papers into the air, which scattered all around them. They quickly separated and started to pick up their clothes. Meanwhile, the female was saying over and over, "We weren't doing anything! We weren't doing anything! We weren't doing anything!" Finally I said, "Really! You weren't doing anything? Then why are you naked?" She looked me dead in the eye and said, "It was hot!" Thankfully another, much older and much more confident teacher came by at this point and took over. I was thoroughly traumatized. Later, I asked the Ass. Principal what happened to the students. She said they had a conference with the parents and the mother of the girl tried to argue that the students weren't doing anything wrong and that it doesn't say anywhere in the school rulebook that students can't have sex. She is right about that. It does not state in the rulebook that students can't have sex at school. Clearly the school needed to add that rule and specifically indicate the locations where sexual activity is forbidden.

ATTACK HELICOPTER PARENT

Ruprecht's father watched the online gradebook carefully all semester as his son's grade hovered around an A. When it dropped below an 89.9% I would immediately get an email asking for clarification as to why his son's grade was now a B, followed by a lengthy explanation/reminder that Ruprecht was on the fast track to Ivy League, and if I gave him a B, it would ruin his perfect GPA and chances at a successful life. I would respectfully give the breakdown of the current grades and assignments, and remind the father that his son really needed to work on his writing skills because his poorly written essays were bringing down his grade. I usually wouldn't get a response to that, although in one email, he took the time to explain to me that, "Frankly in a global economy, your subject matter is irrelevant." (I find this interesting, because in any economy, and any profession, his son would need to speak and write coherently, or else be judged as an uneducated moron, but I digress.)

When the grades finally came out at the end of the semester, Ruprecht had an 88, which is undeniably and unarguably a B. His father flew into action. A barrage of emails started, not just to me, but to the chair of my department. The emails sought justice for Ruprecht, since I had sabotaged his chances at Yale or Harvard or wherever. A meeting was set up with the dad and an administrator. I had to go through every assignment that I had given Ruprecht, and explain the expectations and the resulting grade while my supervisor confirmed that everything was status quo. The father continued to try to find reasons why the B was unfair. He said that he did not agree with my grading policies and that I graded too harshly. The chair told him that he was wrong and asked him to please accept Ruprecht's earned grade graciously. The meeting was promptly ended with a dramatic, "This isn't over."

Next, the father went to the principal. After explaining the entire story to him, he took my side, but the dad was relentless about the unfairness of my essay grading. Instead of telling him to fuck off, the principal set up a panel of other English teachers to look at the work I had graded (for no extra pay, I might add). They all agreed that it was fair and accurate. Some even thought I graded his work too highly. Take *that* Ruprecht's dad.

His next move was to show up in the school parking lot near my car, waiting for me to discuss my grading policies. We argued a bit until I got into my car and drove away. I alerted the school that this man was actually stalking me. They said to let them know if he did anything like that again.

The school year ended and I had forgotten all about Ruprecht and his psycho dad. During Back to School Night the following school year I noticed Ruprecht's dad sitting amongst the parents in my classroom, taking copious notes while I spoke. I definitely thought this was strange since I no longer had his son as a student. He took those notes to the superintendent, claiming that my stated expectations and grading policies did not match my actual grading style.

It is a year later, and the battle continues today. Ruprecht's dad is actually suing the school district claiming that the grade caused his son "severe physical and emotional suffering, along with decreased college admission chances, lost scholarships, and loss of future employment opportunities."

I have had to assemble extensive amounts of information about my grading, lesson plans, samples of other student work, etc. for various school officials but thankfully, they no longer include me in their dealings with Ruprecht's dad.

MOMMY ISSUES

In 10th-grade, we read Homer's *The Odyssey*. Although it is over 500 pages in length, the book itself weighs less than a pound. In 10th-grade, a student is 15 or 16 years old. Any rational person would think it a reasonable request to give a student one copy of the book to take home at night and bring back the next day for use in class. Certainly the school does not have the resources to keep in-class copies for students while giving second copies for at-home use. But this had to be the case for Fritz. His mother insisted that he have two copies, for it was too much of a strain on Fritz's back and arms to carry that 13-ounce book to and fro all the time.

Now I know you're thinking, "Fritz must have a physical ailment which impedes him from carrying books and so this is a reasonable request." I hate to inform you that Fritz's only ailment was his mommy. She insisted that he be given two copies of *The Odyssey*, because it was too heavy for his 15-year-old frame. This isn't the only thing that Fritz's mother insisted upon.

Another thing which Fritz's mother required was a monthly conference with all of her son's teachers to make sure that he had an A in all of his classes. The school has an electronic grade book which posts grades online, so the conferences were quite unnecessary. These conferences became more of a situation where she would badger and bully the teachers who were not "giving" her son an A. Many of these meetings took place in a conference room around a phone, because Fritz's mom was too busy to actually come to the building to meet with us. There would be eight or nine teachers, a guidance counselor, the school psychologist and an assistant principal sitting around a speakerphone. It would go like this:

GUIDANCE COUNSELOR: Okay, Mrs. Nutjarb. We're all here.

VOICE OF FRITZ'S MOM: I'd like to speak to math first. What happened on the quiz you gave two weeks ago?

MATH TEACHER: I'm sorry, you'll have to be more specific.

FRITZ'S MOM: Well, on December 1st you gave a quiz entitled "Formulas Quiz" and my son got a B. I was wondering why.

MATH TEACHER: Well, I don't have his quiz in front of me but I'm assuming that he got a few questions wrong.

FRITZ'S MOM: That is unacceptable. What does he need to do to get an A in your class?

MATH TEACHER: He needs to get higher grades on his tests and quizzes. But he is doing well. He currently has an 88%.

FRITZ'S MOM: You may consider 88% to be doing well but in our family anything below an A is a failure. I'll be keeping in touch through email to determine how we can improve on his grade. I'd like to speak to biology next.

BIOLOGY TEACHER: Yes, hello.

FRITZ'S MOM: Why did Fritz get a zero on the first lab that you did? He told me that you gave him an extension.

This pattern would continue until Fritz's mom thoroughly harassed all of her son's teachers about every grade that wasn't an A. And thank God Fritz got an A in my class, because she complained to the Board of Education five times over his former English teacher who "gave him a B because she doesn't like him."

She also insisted that her son be excused from reading Eli Wiesel's *Night*, a memoir about a young man's experiences in Nazi concentration camps. She said that at fifteen years old he wasn't emotionally ready to handle the subject matter

116

and should be given a text with lighter themes. The problem was that while reading a text, we discuss it in depth and even watch films that connect to the book's themes. So Fritz spent two months sitting in the hallway alone, reading a different selection that his mom approved of. We didn't see much of Fritz during that time for, at his mother's urging, he was not allowed to be present for any part of class which dealt with the Holocaust in any way.

Fritz's mom is not the only parent who had objections to English texts. Many students are forbidden to read certain books due to their parents' religious beliefs. Parents have insisted that their kid be excused from reading *The Catcher in the Rye* because there are curse words and a prostitute in the book (although nothing inappropriate happens). *The Lord of the Flies* is too violent. *1984* is pro-communist. *Of Mice and Men* "uses the lord's name in vain." One student could not read *Brave New World* because it promoted sex outside of marriage. Another could not be present during discussions of the afterlife while reading *Hamlet* because discussing any possibilities other than the Christian outcome of heaven and hell felt blasphemous to her parents. It started out as an innocent conversation about Hamlet pondering the unknown aspects of the afterlife. When other students expressed their feelings about different possible outcomes after death, she started screaming at the class that if we didn't take Jesus into our hearts we would burn in hell. When other kids said they felt insulted by that, she left the room and came to class the next day with a note from her parents explaining that she would need to be excused during open-ended discussions like that from now on. One might think that parents like this would send their kid to a religious school, but instead they burden public servants with their unreasonable demands.

A GREAT MYSTERY

This is a transcript of a parent-teacher conference for Mabel, a smart yet extremely angry girl, who was thrown out of her previous school for constantly starting violent fights.

NOTE: This meeting took place during my lunch period.

ASS. PRINCIPAL: We're here to figure out how we can help Mabel be more successful in her classes.

MABEL'S MOM: Okay.

COUNSELOR: Let's go around and hear from each teacher about Mabel's performance and attitude.

SCIENCE TEACHER: Mabel has a very poor attitude, is extremely rude and will not do any work.

ME: I have the same experience. On the first day of class, I asked the class a question and she announced that no one gave a shit. I spoke to her about it privately and she refused to acknowledge that what she said was inappropriate.

HISTORY TEACHER: Yes, Mabel can be extremely rude and disrespectful. She will not complete any work in class.

ART TEACHER: She never listens to anything I ask her to do. Every time I ask her to take her headphones out she takes them out for a minute and puts them right back in.

ME: I have the same experience. I always feel like she is testing me to see how far she can push me.

COUNSELOR: Maybe she keeps putting the headphones back in because of her A.D.D.

MABEL'S MOM: Yes, Mabel has A.D.D.

ME: I don't think so. It really feels like she can control herself, but refuses to.

HISTORY TEACHER: Can I ask why she isn't in this meeting? Isn't the student usually present?

ASS. PRINCIPAL: We sent for her at the end of last period. I don't know why she isn't here.

MABEL'S MOM: Oh she told me she wouldn't be here.

ASS. PRINCIPAL: Why?

MABEL'S MOM: She said she doesn't care what you have to say.

ASS. PRINCIPAL: Okay. Well, the main reason that this meeting was called was because of Mabel's behavior in math class last week that led to her suspension.

MATH TEACHER: I told Mabel that if she continued to refuse to do work she would have to leave. She said, and I quote, "I don't give a fuck!" I told her to leave class and she said, "Fuck you!" and pushed a bunch of papers off my desk before she left.

MABEL'S MOM: Yes, I got a phone call about that.

COUNSELOR: Okay, does anyone have any ideas about how we can help Mabel be more successful in her classes? Perhaps we can offer extra help? She gets extended time on all assignments because of her A.D.D.

MABEL'S MOM: That's true.

HISTORY TEACHER: But what does that matter if she won't complete any work?

119

COUNSELOR: We just want her to have all the resources she needs to improve. Would you offer extra help?

HISTORY TEACHER: I always offer extra help to my students. They all know that. I am available during my lunch period, before and after school and anytime through email. I don't think Mabel will take advantage of that.

ME: Same here. I am always available if a student needs help.

SCIENCE TEACHER: Me too.

ASS. PRINCIPAL: Okay, we'll make sure Mabel knows that extra help is available. Does anyone have any other insights into why Mabel is not able to perform the work?

SCIENCE TEACHER: Mabel has the intelligence and the skills to complete the work, she just refuses to.

HISTORY TEACHER: I agree.

ME: Yes, me too.

MABEL'S MOM: I just don't know what to do. I don't know why she's acting like this.

COUNSELOR: I'm sure her A.D.D. has something to do with it.

ME: Do you mind if I ask you a question?

MABEL'S MOM: No, go ahead.

ME: When you found out that Mabel was being suspended for cursing at a teacher, what happened when she got home from school?

MABEL'S MOM: What do you mean?

ME: Were there any consequences?

MABEL'S MOM (*after a blank stare*): Like what?

ME: Does she still have a phone?

MABEL'S MOM: Yes.

ME: Who pays the bill?

MABEL'S MOM: Me.

ME: Okay, well maybe you could take away her phone.

MABEL'S MOM (*with a bright smile*): She'd never let me do that.

Awkward silence

ME: Oh.

Awkward silence

ASS. PRINCIPAL: Does anyone have anything to add? Okay, we'll let Mabel know about the resources that are available to her.

MABEL'S MOM: Thanks.

PARENTING DISORDER

Bob didn't come to class very often. If he did show up, he was usually 45 minutes late, and he would promptly put his head down and go to sleep. I tried everything with Bob; I yelled at him, slipped papers under his face, I even rang a cowbell in his ear. Finally, I pulled him into the hallway for a chat. I asked him to be completely honest and tell me what his deal was. He said that he didn't care about school. He only cared about his computer, and he stayed up until four or five in the morning playing games. I asked if his parents were aware of this. He said yes. I explained that if he wanted a future in computers he would probably need a degree and that he'd need to graduate high school first. He said he understood what I was saying, and he'd think about it.

I kept getting emails from Bob's mom explaining that he had an autism spectrum disorder, and that this prevented him from being able to pay attention in class, ask for help, express himself in writing, complete his homework or even care about school. I explained that if Bob showed up more, I would do everything I could to accommodate him, although I wasn't sure how I was supposed to get around the whole writing thing, seeing as how this was an Honors English class. It didn't matter because Bob still wasn't coming to class.

An interesting change occurred in the middle of the semester. I received an email from the assistant principal stating that Bob had been put on probation and that if he did anything wrong such as come to class late, sleep in class or refuse to do work, he would be withdrawn from school. Well Bob was a new man. He came to class early every day for two weeks. He was awake and alert, added insightful information to class discussions and completed every assignment, both in and out of class. He also wrote one of the best essays of all the students in the class, even though his mother argued that his disorder prevented him from being able to express himself in written form. After the two weeks had ended, Bob was back to his old ways. I asked him why he wasn't performing at the high level I had seen in the previous two weeks. He was rather matter of fact when he stated that, "The two-week probation is up. They're not throwing me out, so I don't have to care anymore." Clearly this proved that Bob was capable of doing quality work and was simply choosing not to. If only he had a little discipline and a few consequences, he would do what he was supposed to.

I brought this up at the meeting we had with Bob, Bob's parents, the assistant principal, the head of the Special Education department, the school psychologist and Bob's special education case worker. Bob's parents had brought a lawyer to the meeting as well because they said that the school was robbing their son of his right to a free public education. The school said that they were doing everything they could to assist Bob, but that if he wasn't willing to do any work, they couldn't help him. The lawyer said that the school was discriminating against Bob because of his autism. The school psychologist explained that if Bob really had such a high level of autism, the school was not equipped to handle that and that they would happily refer him to an alternative school in the district.

I was happy to share my interesting observation with the group. I said that I found it fascinating that Bob was the ideal student for two weeks when there was an actual disciplinary consequence. I explained in detail the way Bob acted, and even what he said about not needing to care after the two weeks were up. I also told them that he was up all night playing on the computer and that is why he is always so tired. No one said anything. The parents, their lawyer and their son were completely silent with blank looks on their faces. The psychologist and case worker had big smiles.

The assistant principal said that this was a very interesting piece of information and seemed to prove that Bob was quite capable. The mom turned to Bob and said, "Maybe we should try taking your computer away." Bob looked at her with contempt and replied, "Don't you remember? You tried that once and it didn't work." The mom shrugged her shoulders. There was more silence. The lawyer continued his argument as though that little exchange never took place. The meeting yielded no solution. I didn't see Bob for the rest of the marking period. A few days before the end of the semester I received the following thread of emails:

From: Bob's mom

To: Bob's counselor

Cc: All of Bob's teachers

Subject: Bob

Dear Bob's counselor,

I'm wondering if you can help Bob get any work turned in before the end of the marking period next week. He is failing all of his classes and does not know what to do. He does not understand what is required of him in class. He comes home and doesn't understand what his homework is or how to do it. I am particularly interested in getting his English grade up to a D, because he did complete a few assignments. Can you help him?

I don't know what to say about his other classes. Is there any way for him to pass?

Bob's mom

From: Bob's counselor

To: Bob's mom

Cc: All of Bob's teachers

Subject: RE: Bob

Good Afternoon,

At this point Bob has to ask the teachers what he can do. All of his teachers have offered him help but he won't take the offers. The end of the marking period is in 2 days. His English teacher has really been trying to help him but he won't let her. Everyone has been trying to help but he won't take the help. He is doing quite well in Chemistry, because he comes to class and does the work. After the deadline was up for his contract with the assistant principal, he wouldn't cooperate with his teachers and he refused to do any work. My hands are really tied on this because the teachers have been trying to help him and Bob felt that the contract was up and he didn't have to do any work. His English teacher included you on the last email, telling you how he would not do any work on his research paper or even take a quiz. It appears that when Bob decides to do any work in any class he will.

Have A Nice Day.

Bob's counselor

From: Bob's mom

To: All of Bob's teachers and his counselor

Subject: RE: Bob

Dear Bob's counselor,

I know that Bob's performance in school has not been

great. But as a parent, I feel that more needs to be done to help Bob get the appropriate education to which he has a right. Bob has an autism spectrum disorder and is NOT willfully refusing teachers' help and refusing to do work, although it may appear that he is. We believe that he is actually learning the material in the classes he attends, and needs an alternative way to show that he understands the content. It seems that his poor work-study habits are causing his grades to be low - not his knowledge of the subject matter. We would like to request that he be granted accommodations that make work-load adjustments, based on the following recommendations from his Neuropsychological Evaluation.

Neuropsychological Evaluation

(Note to reader: I have eliminated an enormous amount of this THIRTY ONE PAGE document)

RECOMMENDATIONS

1. Individualized selection of teachers. It is strongly recommended that Bob and his parents select appropriate teachers for the coming year. Due to his social disorder, a classroom format that emphasizes group or cooperative learning is likely to be the most difficult and stressful modality of learning. He will also require a classroom teaching model that allows him to work independently (i.e., not in groups), for learning, studying, and producing work output.

2. Teachers practice social skills. In order to support social development, Bob will require explicit training from his teachers in social skills, as well as specific mechanisms to ensure that the skills taught in training generalize to real life settings.

3) Bob will require a social skills training program for students with social learning disorders. As an example, this type of training program would explicitly teach Bob how to accurately read nonverbal communication, such as

facial expressions and body language. If the school does not have this type of program, materials may be provided to assist in the creation of one.

4) Teachers role play. Social skills training should be integrated as much as possible across school settings. This will require the training of teachers, and identification of ways for Bob to build social skills within the classroom. As much as possible, teachers should role play and plan with Bob about appropriate ways of interacting within these specific activities, and then monitor his performance and provide feedback as needed. Bob's teachers must be aware of the social skill that he is being taught in training each week. That way, the same social skill can be reinforced throughout the week across the multiple settings of Bob's life.

6) People watching. Bob's parents and teachers may also work towards improving his social awareness in real life by "people watching" with him. For example, teachers may watch a social interaction or group with Bob and discuss the nature of the interactions, the emotions of the different people, how they are related, the facial expressions and body language being used, etc.

7) Accommodations in class for Bob's social deficits include the following:

i) While Bob works on learning appropriate social skills during group projects with peers, provide other ways for him to learn the academic information.

ii) If Bob makes remarks that seem rude or disrespectful, teachers should not try to correct or discipline Bob but explain the effect of his words later in a nonjudgmental manner. Do not assume that disrespect was intended.

iii) Teachers should be aware of the possibility that Bob is becoming over-stimulated and should allow a break from the social or cognitive activity of the environment. In addition, Bob should be taught how to request assistance at those times and strategies for soliciting the teacher's attention in order to request a break.

8) Recommended accommodations for the classroom for Bob include the following:

a) Visual Schedules: As much as possible, provide Bob with advanced notice of changes in classroom schedules or routines.

b) Frequent modeling of planning, organizational skills, problem-solving, and emotional self-regulation is recommended. For example, teachers can explicitly model their own thinking when confronted with a multi-step task that requires organization or planning.

c) Teachers should incorporate Bob's personal interests into teaching or relate new information to his personal interests in some way, to capture his focus and motivation in the classroom.

d) Preferential classroom seating. Bob should be able to choose a seat near the teacher's desk to maximize his ability to attend and comprehend the teacher.

e) Lessons in organization. Teachers should help with organizing Bob's desk, notebooks, and locker.

f) Individual Check-ins. When assignments are given teachers should have an individual conversation with Bob to make sure he understands the task, and help him develop an organized, step-by-step strategy for completing the task. Break larger tasks and assignments into sub steps, generating time lines for completion of each step, and monitoring progress. This should be presented to him as an opportunity to discuss his thoughts and ideas, and not as an additional academic requirement.

g) Homework review. Teachers should review homework assignments with Bob before he leaves school each day, making sure he understands the assignments, takes home the correct materials, and has a strategy or plan for completing each task. Provide Bob with individual reminders to turn in completed work.

h) Extra time. Extra time to complete assignments and tests will be required.

i) Copy of teacher's notes. Bob should receive a copy of the teacher's notes to minimize note-taking. When required to copy information from the board, teachers must ensure that Bob has accurately copied the information.

j) For self-esteem: Bob will benefit from having teachers acknowledge a good performance, and from their ability to create situations which will facilitate success. In addition, ensuring that Bob receives ample opportunity to excel in areas of strength will be essential.

9. Accommodations for standardized testing:

a) At least 50% extended time on tests.

b) Preferential seating, away from auditory and visual distracters, and in a smaller group environment is recommended.

c) Responding directly in the test booklet, rather than on the bubble answer sheet, is recommended due to Bob's visual organization weakness.

10. Individualized Teaching of Executive Functioning Skills. Teachers should explicitly teach the learning of skills that other students may learn on their own, such as organization skills, study strategies, self-monitoring skills, good homework management strategies, and note-taking strategies.

a) Goals of individualized teaching may include assistance with organization of materials. Bob will need assistance and check-ins to make sure he is getting maximum benefit from such a planner. He should be assisted in setting up his notebooks for each class, and making sure he has a system for clearly recording and keeping track of assignments.

b) Bob is likely to benefit from learning to organize information for learning. Thus, he will need to be taught strategies such as outlining, organizing related information into meaningful categories or patterns, linking new information to previous knowledge, summarizing, and developing mnemonic devices.

c) Given Bob's piecemeal / parts-oriented processing style, teachers should do activities that encourage relating the parts to the whole, or that focus on the "big picture."

d) Bob will require assistance with the organizational requirements of reading independently for meaning. He should therefore be taught efficient reading strategies, such as skimming for meaning, using a highlighter to focus on main points, and developing outlines to help him organize the information.

e) In written language, Bob requires assistance with generating ideas, and organizing, sequencing, and prioritizing his ideas for essays and writing assignments.

f) Re-teaching, in which Bob must teach new information to someone else, will be a useful tool for reinforcing Bob's knowledge.

g) School personnel should read the following book in order to learn to accommodate executive dysfunction and teaching executive functioning skills: Executive Skills in Children and Adolescents: A Practical Guide to Assessment and Intervention, by Peg Dawson and Richard Guare (2004, The Guilford Press).

No one responded to this email and Bob failed all of his classes. At the end of the summer, I received the following email:

From: Bob's mom

To: Bob's English teacher

Subject: Bob's English grade

Hi,

This is Bob's mom. I was wondering if you could pass Bob for the previous year. We just got his schedule for next year, and see that he will have to repeat your class. His father and I feel that this will be detrimental to Bob's self-esteem. We believe he has gained a great amount of knowledge from being present in your class but is unable to provide evidence of that knowledge. Please consider passing him. He is very bright and we wouldn't want his English grade to ruin his confidence.

Thank you,

Bob's mom

I thought about answering this email by explaining that her argument was flawed because Bob was rarely present in class, but instead I ignored it and awaited the interesting stories about Bob that would continue to be discussed in the office the following year.

Eventually, Bob just stopped coming to school altogether and never graduated. I ran into his mother a few years later and she happily told me that he was working for a very successful internet start-up, making "well over six figures!" I really wanted to be happy for Bob, but the fact that he was making three times as much money as me, without even a high school diploma, at the age of 20... Yeah I was admittedly a bit bitter. Fuck Bob.

LOW SELF-ESTEEM

Gus wasn't a very conspicuous student. He sat in the back of the classroom, did his work, and was pretty quiet. One day, towards the end of the semester, a stinky smoke bomb was lit near my classroom. No one had any information about who did it. Soon after, I saw a flicker of light coming from the back of my room. I tried to ignore it, but then I realized it was a flame. I walked over and saw Gus flicking a lighter. He did not stop when I approached him. I told him to give me the lighter. He asked when he would get it back. I said never. He was mad. I wrote him up. Nothing happened.

Naturally, after this incident I was wary of Gus. And after this incident, Gus displayed some rather strange behavior. He started to write very bizarre essays, which had nothing to do with the assigned topic. He thought his essays were hilarious. He began to fail the class because of this. I took Gus aside and explained that if he did this type of writing on his final exam, he would undoubtedly fail. He just shrugged his shoulders. I contacted the school psychologist. Nothing happened.

During his final exam, Gus was laughing hysterically as he wrote his essay and I knew what was coming. His essay included the following lines (keep in mind that this essay was supposed to be about the nature of success), "I kill people all the time. Out on the street, I see an enemy torturing a poor child with a stun gun, so I shoot him in the head. Another example of when I killed a man was just last week as I was walking home from the psycho ward. After finally being released, I began running in the middle of the road drinking beer and shooting my shotgun at people. I then stopped to admire the police as they shot a man for armed robbery."

He handed this in with plenty of time to spare and sat at his desk with a huge smile on his face. I read his essay in horror. The essay prompt asked the students to form an argument based on non-fiction articles from the test itself. Nowhere did it say to include personal, fictional and/or psychotic examples. I took Gus into the hallway. This is what transpired:

ME: Gus, I am very worried about you. Are you aware that if you hand this in, you will get a zero?

GUS: Yes.

ME: Okay, then why did you write it?

GUS: Because it's hilarious.

ME: Okay. But I think that you should sit down and write another essay. You still have time.

GUS: No. I like this essay.

ME: Okay, as long as you're aware that you will fail. You did not address the prompt at all. I'm not even the one who will grade it, and the teachers who do will be using a very specific rubric. If you don't attempt to answer the given question, you will get a zero.

GUS: (*Laughing*) Okay.

A few days later, we all had to evacuate the building and stand in the snow for over an hour because someone had set the boy's bathroom on fire. There was no footage of who set the fire from the security cameras because there was too much smoke and there weren't any witnesses. But an administrator remembered my write-up about a boy playing with a lighter and had the wisdom to call him into her office. He immediately admitted that he had set the fire. In fact, he was quite proud of it. When asked for an explanation he said, "I just really like to light stuff on fire. I like to watch things burn." It was clear that we needed to call Gus's

132

parents in for a meeting about their son's psychological issues. But first, Gus needed to be arrested.

The cops went to Gus's house and arrested him. He spent the night in jail. His parents came in for a meeting with the school administrators and psychologists a few days later. You would think that they would be disturbed by their son's behavior, and concerned with his psychological well-being, right? Well, what Gus's parents were more concerned with was his failing grade on his English final. According to them, Gus had always been insecure about his writing and he came home very excited after the exam. He said that I read his essay and told him it was a real winner, and that he would definitely receive an A. Then when he found out that he failed he felt betrayed, and his self-esteem suffered. According to them, this is why he set the school on fire.

Believe it or not, we actually had to take this seriously. In any other real-world setting, anyone would say to these parents, "Are you fucking kidding me? Your kid set the school on fire because of low self-esteem? Get the fuck outta here!" But we have to be professional and civil. So it was explained to Gus's parents that Gus's version of the story was false. He was told that he would fail with the essay he had written, and was even given a chance to re-write it. They didn't believe us; they chose instead to believe their arsonist son.

Gus's parents requested to see a copy of Gus's essay with the grading rubric. Another conference was scheduled specifically for this reason. His parents argued that the essay deserved at least a B according to the rubric we used. They did not mention the fire Gus had set or the violent and disturbing nature of the essay he wrote. According to them, Gus earned at least a B on his English final. They refused to discuss the arson until this was attended to. We all held fast to the grade the essay had originally received and tried to get them to focus on the fire. We even showed them pictures of the damage Gus had caused. They tried to ignore us and said they would be going to the school board with their grade change request. We explained that Gus was about to be expelled from school for arson. Their response was that they were getting a lawyer to fight that too, since it was our (my) fault (you know, the whole low self-esteem thing).

Next I received an email from a "pupil personnel worker."

From: Pupil Personnel Worker

To: English Teacher

Cc: Other important people

Subject: Student concern

Hello. I have just spoken to Gus's parents about the fire setting incident last week. Needless to say, they are very upset with the whole situation.

I read the post in the communication log about the final exam essay. Parents say they spoke to you about the essay. They said the situation was explained as to why he responded the way he did and that you agreed to change his grade to an A (their words). Please put a copy of the essay in my mailbox located in the main office.

I don't see documentation regarding the parent conference involving the "explanation" and the grade change. Would you please document the contact? I need to be able to report the whole incident because the parents plan to share the situation at the investigative hearing.

Thanks,

Pupil Personnel Worker

Gus's parents lied. Here is the answer that my supervisor gave for me:

From: English Teacher's Supervisor

To: Pupil Personnel Worker

Cc: Other important people

Subject: Re: Student concern

Dear Pupil Personnel Worker,

Neither Gus's teacher nor I agreed to change Gus's grade. In fact, I told the parents that I would consult with my district supervisor regarding the essay and its content. In that conversation with the district supervisor, he noted several points (similar to the ones I attempted to convey to Gus's parents):

·The essay does not present itself seriously due to the overtly fabricated material. [The parents, however, argued that Gus was very serious and bragged about the good job he had done.]

·The thinking is weak and not representative of an honors student.

·The essay does not demonstrate mastery of thinking and does not engage in a serious way with the task.

·The essay engages only in a crude manner, using fabricated material that is violent and inappropriate.

All that said, the issue comes down to whether the student gets a "0" because most of the content is fabricated, which renders the essay irrelevant; or does he get a score point of an "F" because he does make some attempt to answer the question, even if the detail is erroneous, and he demonstrates some mastery of writing. A score of "F" would not change his course grade overall.

Gus's dad was insistent that the essay was an excellent work of fiction and that it be given an A. I made it clear that I understood why it received a "0" but would seek my supervisor's input. My supervisor agreed that it is a gray area, and he could see the argument for either a "0" due to the irrelevant examples, or an "F" because of the few existing, though weak examples. I am reluctant to change the grade because it undermines the process that an independent body of teachers used to assign a grade to the paper. They determined that the response was irrelevant. I would also like to add that I was very uncomfortable at several points during the conversation with Gus's parents. It seems that they were in denial about the real problem. Gus is obviously very bright. However, he chose to use some rather graphic and disturbing images in his essay, images that he made up, which renders them even more troubling. Gus's dad continued to make the point that Gus was crushed to learn that he had earned a "0" but Gus had a mocking attitude all along. His parents make a passionate plea, but their pleas seem to belie all of the evidence that their son is leaving.

Please contact me if you have any further questions regarding this troubling matter.

Thanks,

English Department Supervisor

Gus was "on leave" until his hearing with the school board was finished. The school board decided to expel him. Gus's parents tried to fight this with a lawyer, but when they saw the fight wasn't going anywhere, they withdrew him from school before he could be expelled and enrolled him in an alternative school. The next semester when I got my class roster I was shocked to see Gus's name on it. That's right- Gus was allowed back to school. I was expected to teach Gus once again, as though nothing had happened.

For once, instead of just accepting it, I decided to fight. I spoke to his counselor, who agreed that it would not be in the best interest of either of us to be placed together again. There were many other teachers who did not know Gus's history and he could have a fresh start. The counselor just wanted to give

Gus's mom a call to let her know that his schedule was being switched around. Clearly she would be happy about the switch, given the fact that I caused such low self-esteem for her son last year (bad enough to turn him into an arsonist!) Well, common sense took a backseat for this one.

Gus's mom argued with the counselor. The counselor tried to remain firm, but I could see she was breaking under the pressure of the mother's contentions. She handed the phone to me and whispered, "She wants to speak with you." I took the phone and said hello. She merely responded with a cold, "Hi." Then there was silence, for an awkward while. So I spoke.

"As you've heard, I think it would be in everyone's best interest if Gus and I avoided working together again, given our history." There was a long pause and an even longer sigh. "I don't agree," the mother said. "Okay," I responded. "I just feel that, given our history, any issues that may come up in the future, regarding grades for example, might bring up the past. And I don't think that would be healthy for Gus." (Basically I was trying to say that I didn't want to be blamed for giving Gus a low grade and causing more blows to his self-esteem because of what he did the year before.) "Yeah I see what you're saying," she replied. "But I just feel that removing him from your class, when he has already seen your name on his schedule will be really bad for him right now. He'll feel rejected. Plus, he has a friend in your class. And he doesn't have a lot of friends." (Gee, I wonder why…) I continued to calmly state my argument and she continued to angrily disagree with me. Finally, I said I would talk to my supervisor about it and see what we could work out. I just wanted to get off the phone with her because she was sucking my soul out through my ear.

The chair of my department took my side. "It's not up to the mother where the kid is placed. There are plenty of other teachers and there is no reason for him to have you again." Thank God someone had common sense. But first, she needed to get the schedule change cleared with the Ass. Principal. A week went by and I heard nothing. I continued to have Gus in my class, and he wasn't any more pleasant than before. Finally, I went to see the Ass. Principal myself. I rehashed the entire scenario and waited for her reply. Her answer was that she agreed with Gus's mother. I felt like I was losing my mind. I took a deep breath and said, "I never question any decisions of the administration. But in this case, this is a matter of safety and comfort. As a teacher, don't I deserve to be comfortable in my own classroom?"

She replied, "Of course you do. But did Gus threaten you *directly*?"

"No, but he played with a lighter in my class, then set the building on fire, and his parents blamed *me*!"

"But did he threaten you *directly*?"

"Did he threaten *my life*? No…"

"Then you really don't have a right to say that you don't feel safe with him in your classroom."

I tried to argue a bit more and she said she would go to the principal for the final decision. I received an email a few days later saying that the principal also agreed with Gus's mother and that was that.

But the fun didn't end there. From day one of my second year with Gus, he was difficult and practically screaming for attention. First he tried writing inappropriate things in his classwork. Then he constantly interrupted me while I spoke. When that didn't get a reaction, he started cursing at other students. Finally, I decided to take a more honest approach and I asked Gus to stay after class for a talk. I told him exactly how I felt. I said that I never got an explanation as to why he set the school on fire the year before and explained that I felt hurt that he allowed his parents to blame me for his actions. He agreed and seemed to understand how I felt. I asked why he did what he did and he said that he did not remember because he had blacked out. He shared many alarming things about his mental health, including the large amount of psychiatric medication that he was on and the fact that he never took them regularly (which can be very dangerous). He also explained that he often has the urge to act violently towards himself or others, has outbursts of violence (like setting things on fire or beating people up) and then blacks out. When he wakes up, he said, he is usually in the middle of the woods near his house or in the gutter with no recollection of what had happened. I told him that this was very upsetting information and I urged him to speak to the school psychologist. He said he would and apologized, genuinely, for his behavior.

Although Gus seemed to tell me that information in confidence, I knew I was entering an uncomfortable gray area that no teacher ever wants to be in. I determined that what Gus had told me was distressing enough to contact the administration about. *Here we go again*, I thought to myself as I walked to the Ass. Principal's office to meet with Gus's counselor and the school psychologist. I told them everything that he told me, including his alarming comments about having violent tendencies and blackouts. The school psychologist said she would speak to his mother about taking him to a psychiatric center. She did speak to the mother and the mother said that the psychologist whom they recently brought him to determined that he was fine and she ended the discussion there.

Next, Gus started showing up to class stoned out of his mind. Not only did he have bright red eyes, he stunk like pot and he couldn't keep his head off of the desk. I asked to speak with him and he admitted, although in confidence, that he had been smoking pot in school every day and drinking heavily on the weekends. I explained my worries about his mixing drugs and alcohol with prescriptions, especially given his violent tendencies. He just shrugged and left the room. Again, I was in an uncomfortable position. I wanted Gus to be able to confide things in me, but I couldn't let this information go without informing the administration. I sent out the following email:

From: English Teacher

To: Ass. Principal

Cc: School psychologist, counselor

Subject: Student concern

I am writing to express my concern over Gus. He has been coming to class with very red, irritated eyes and he has his head down most of the class, regardless of efforts to wake him up. His eyes were so red and swollen that he could barely open them. He admitted to smoking marijuana, and mixing that with his medication, this could be very harmful to his well-being. I don't know if there is anything that can be done, but I want to make sure that everyone is aware of what is going on.

The Ass. Principal said that several other teachers and even a security guard complained that Gus smelled like marijuana and they had already called his mother. The mother said that in response, she asked her son if he was smoking marijuana, and he said no, so she believed him. Yet now that they had a teacher saying that he actually admitted to it, they would urge her to get him help. I wrote back and reminded her that he had told me that information in confidence. The Ass. Principal assured me that they would not use my name. Yet when they told the mother that Gus admitted he had been smoking marijuana and drinking, she insisted on knowing who the teacher was. They refused to tell her but asked her to consider the information instead. She said that she needed to know who the teacher was in order to take the claim seriously. They begged her to take him for help, but she repeated the fact that he told her that he does not do drugs.

Gus continued to come to class stoned. I was told not to let him sleep in class and to ask him to go to the nurse. I sent him out many times and then checked with the nurse to confirm that he showed up, and of course he didn't. Instead, he would go across the street to smoke more pot in an alley. When I told the Ass. Principal about this, her answer was, "Well, what do you expect? You didn't call security to take him there."

Gus started to make a theatrical production out of his sleeping in class. He would snore loudly and drool extensively onto his desk. I had to go to extreme lengths to wake him up. I called security to take him to the nurse, as I was instructed to do. They escorted him to the nurse and brought him back five minutes later saying that he had very low blood pressure (which is often caused by taking drugs). Then he went back to snoring and drooling. After that I just let him sleep, because it was preferable to his disrupting the class by having to call security or fighting with him to stay awake.

On the last day of class, Gus asked me what the prompt was for one of the writing assignments that he missed. When I told him, he responded with, "That's it? That's stupid." At this point, I had had enough. I told him that he was rude, his opinion was not welcomed and that he was lucky I would even accept his late work. This is the paper that he turned in:

"I asked my teacher to clarify the question and I got the rudest response

I've ever received from an unprovoked teacher. I don't mind getting bitched at when it's deserved, but there's no excuse for such rude and hostile behavior coming from a teacher. I would recommend getting help if this continues for it's unsafe in a high school setting for a teacher to repeatedly try to provoke their students."

I had to hold myself back from chasing after the kid. A few days later I received the following letter,

Dear Ms. Morris,

Thank you. You are an amazing teacher.

I'm sorry for the trouble I've caused.

I promise it was in no way intentional.

Sincerely,

Gus

A RACIST PHASE

As you have heard about several times, on the first day of school, I ask the class to introduce themselves. When Conchita stood up to share about herself, Waldo shocked me with his response.

CONCHITA: My name is Conchita and I'm fifteen. I was born-

WALDO (*facing the opposite direction, under his breath*): Shut up.

ME: Excuse me. That was very rude.

WALDO: I don't care. I don't like Mexicans.

ME: What is wrong with you? You can't just say things like that. Please keep your opinions to yourself or I will ask you to leave. Conchita, please continue.

CONCHITA: Okay. I was born in Mexico and moved here when-

Waldo now turns around and looks Conchita right in the face.

WALDO: I said shut the fuck up!

CONCHITA: Fuck you!

ME: Okay Waldo, you need to leave. Get out now.

Waldo grabs a glass iced tea bottle off another student's desk, takes Conchita by the neck and shoves her up against the wall.

WALDO: I will break this fucking bottle and cut you!

ME: Bernie, run and get security! Waldo, let her go right now!

Waldo lets Conchita go and angrily sits back in his seat. Security comes and removes him from class and we awkwardly continue introducing ourselves.

Later that day I met with the Ass. Principal to discuss the situation. She explained that they have had several issues in the past with Waldo threatening other students, but that because he never acts on it, they can't do much to punish him. She called his mother and put the phone on speaker.

ASS. PRINCIPAL: Hello Ma'am. I am calling again to discuss Waldo's behavior.

WALDO'S MOM: Oh my. It's the first day and he's done something already?

ASS. PRINCIPAL: Yes, something very serious. He threatened a student.

WALDO'S MOM: Oh dear.

ASS. PRINCIPAL: He threatened to cut a female student because she is Mexican.

WALDO'S MOM: Yes, he's sort of going through this little racist phase right now. I'll talk to him about it.

ASS. PRINCIPAL: Please do. This is unacceptable. We will have to suspend him again.

WALDO'S MOM: Oh my. I understand. We'll have a little chat when he gets home. Thank you so much for calling.

Waldo was eventually expelled for threatening an African-American student with a knife, so I didn't have to deal with him for very long. Hopefully, he's outgrown his "little racist phase."

I DEDUCT POINTS IF I DON'T LIKE YOUR FACE

I was called into the office of the chair of the department one day. A parent called for a conference and she wanted to brief me on the situation before we went to the actual meeting.

DEPT. HEAD: This is a rough one. This parent says that you gave her son a B because you don't like him.

ME: But that's ridiculous.

DEPT. HEAD: I know. I told her that. I explained that you are a very trustworthy and fair teacher and that if her son got a B, it's because that is what he earned. But she wouldn't let it go and has called a meeting.

ME: Well, what is she saying? What leads her to believe that I don't like her son? I really did treat him like everyone else.

DEPT. HEAD: I know. She has brought in particular assignments and has pointed out each point deduction, saying that it is nitpicky and that you only deducted those points because you don't like him.

ME: Are you kidding me?

DEPT. HEAD: And there's something else...

ME: Yeah?

144

DEPT. HEAD: She claims that you threw a paper at her son.

ME: What?

DEPT. HEAD: The son has said that you were handing back papers and you threw his at him.

ME: That's ridiculous.

DEPT. HEAD: I know.

ME: Sometimes I slide the paper across the desk but-

DEPT. HEAD: There is no need to justify that.

ME: Okay.

DEPT. HEAD: And there's something else.

ME: Oh boy...

DEPT. HEAD: She said that her son said you told him you don't like his face.

ME: What?

DEPT. HEAD: I know.

ME: That's insane.

DEPT. HEAD: I know.

ME: I don't understand why this is happening *now*. I haven't even had her son since last year.

DEPT. HEAD: Yeah, she just came up with this now, which makes it a lot less legitimate. I think it is because he is doing poorly in some of his other classes, and his GPA is going down, so she is looking for ways to bring it up. You're not the only teacher she's doing this to.

ME: So isn't it obvious that her argument has no merit if she is doing the same thing to other teachers?

DEPT. HEAD: Yes, but the school still has to take her complaints seriously.

I denied everything and his mother continued to fight with the school board for several years over her son's grade. I never received a follow-up so I don't know if they gave her what she wanted. But I wouldn't be surprised.

ASSAULT WITH A HILARIOUS WEAPON

A mother came to school looking for her daughter. She had recently lost custody and was not allowed to see her (keep reading to find out why.) She stomped into the main office and demanded to see her daughter. The secretaries informed her that her kid had recently transferred to another school, which was true. The mother accused the secretaries of lying and insisted on seeing her daughter, or else she would be forced to take action. The secretaries told her, once again, that the girl no longer attended this school. The woman swiped all of the items on every desk in the office onto the floor. She took the potted plants and smashed them onto the ground. She kicked the desk of the secretary nearest to her and screamed, "Give me my daughter!"

While the poor secretaries begged her to calm down, the woman took out a backscratcher and a Windex bottle full of hot sauce. She tried to spray one of them with the hot sauce, but it was too thick. Instead, she unscrewed the bottle and tried to fling the sauce. She gave up in frustration and hurled the empty bottle at the secretary's head. Next, she started to chase another secretary with the backscratcher. At this point, a group of teachers restrained the woman, who howled like a rabid animal. The woman was arrested for assault with a (hilarious) weapon.

JUICY FRUIT'S MOM

I had a student who insisted on being called the name of a brand of chewing gum. To conceal his identity, I'll call him "Juicy Fruit" instead. Juicy Fruit refused to take his headphones off and did almost nothing in class. Needless to say, he was failing and therefore, would not be graduating. When his mom found this out, she decided to blame *me*. She sent me the following email a few days before graduation:

```
To: Ms. Morris

From: Juicy Fruit's Mom

Subject: not gonna gradiate

i just found out my son not gonna gradiate because
of your class, why he not pass your class??
```

In my response, I explained to her that no matter what tactic I tried, her son refused to learn. I also reminded her that I had called her many times and left messages throughout the year to discuss her son's failure. She knew all year that he wasn't going to graduate.

She didn't answer but paid me a surprise visit instead. I was in the middle of lecturing Juicy Fruit's class when his mom burst through the door and yelled, "Are you Ms. Morris?"

I had never seen this woman before and it was quite alarming. I jumped and grabbed my chest. A student screamed at the top of her lungs. "It's okay," I told the class. "Yes, I'm Ms. Morris. Can I help you?" Without leaving the doorway, she yelled, "I need to talk to you *now*!"

"I'm in the middle of teaching a class. Can we speak afterward?"

"When's that?"

"In about twenty minutes. Why don't you come back then?"

She had a very sarcastic tone as she replied, "No I think I'm gonna stay and lurn somethin." And with that she sat down in an empty seat in the front row. "Ma'am please," I said. "Please wait for me in the hallway." She crossed her arms and replied, "Naw. Im'ma be *lurnin* something." I tried to continue as if nothing had happened.

"Okay... so absurdism is the belief that nothing can explain or rationalize human existence. Does everyone understand?"

"Oooo I'm *lurnin* stuff," Juicy Fruit's mom called out. I attempted to ignore her.

"Class, how does this theory..."

"Look at me! I'm *lurnin* things!"

I continued to disregard her behavior.

"How does this theory relate to the book?" A few students raised their hands. So did Juicy Fruit's mom. In fact, she started to wave her hand frantically and make noises. I called on a student, but she cut in.

"Yeah, I got a question. How do I get to *pass* this class?"

"Well, you would need to turn in at least a few assignments. Your son did not complete a single assignment all year." Juicy's Fruit's mom looked outraged. She spun around towards where her son was sitting and yelled, "That true?" Her son replied, "No. I did the makeup work. She never graded it."

She turned back to me. "He did the makeup work!"

"I did not receive a single assignment. That is a lie."

She turned back to her son. "You lyin?"

"No. I put it in her mailbox." She turned back to me.

"He put it in ya mailbox!"

"No, he did not. Please go into the hallway so we can discuss this privately." She got up and turned to her son. "When you get home Im'ma kill you!"

"Okay class, open your books and read. Ma'am, let's go in the hallway. Lancelot, call security."

In the hallway, Juicy Fruit's mom yelled at me that my class was stupid and that I should pass her son and that he shouldn't have to stay in school longer because of me. I tried to defend myself. Thankfully security finally showed up. They removed Juicy Fruit's mom from the hallway and dealt with her while I finished teaching my class. No one knows how she got into the building.

Juicy Fruit did some kind of "credit recovery program" and graduated with everyone else. His mom was the loudest and proudest in the crowd.

FROM THE FRONTLINES

Part 2

I asked a group of elementary, middle and high school teachers to describe the most challenging, absurd or outrageous interaction they have had with a parent. This is what I received:

"A parent phoned me at school and yelled at me that her daughter had a bruise and that she's never had a bruise before."

"One of my 5th graders kept falling asleep in my class every day for a week. I called home asking after his health and the dad said, 'Oh that's because I've let him stay up until 1 o'clock watching videos on his iPhone.' Oh, of course, how silly of me!"

"A parent with crazy eyes barged into the school, opened my classroom door and demanded to have a conference immediately. I looked around my class and said, 'Are these kids are invisible? Please come back when you schedule a proper conference.' That lady harassed me all year though I never had ANY issues with her son."

"A student asked me if I was going to cheer for Mexico in the World Cup and my reply was, 'No, I'm cheering for Team USA.' The next day I was called into the principal's office because a parent was accusing me of being racist against Mexicans."

"A parent complained that her son spent too much time with girls and did 'girl things' in the class and didn't have any male friends. Mind you this was a small school and he was the only boy in the previous year's class. I suggested a boy playdate and she told me they were too busy. The second-semester conference began with this same mom complaining that her son is too rough now that he was playing with boys more."

"During a parent conference a father gave me step by step, play by play details on how he found his wife in bed with another woman. I had to pretend I was crying because I was laughing so hard."

"The parent of one of my kindergarten students wrote me a note saying that her son is learning to be a doctor so I should refer to him as Doc."

"I called a parent at 10:30 on a Tuesday and asked for her help with her son's behavior and she said, 'I don't call you on the weekends, so you don't call me during the weekdays. He's *your* problem!'"

"I had a drunk mother angry that her daughter made a 93."

"A student lost her workbook and the mother was irate at having to buy a new one. The mother was in the front office screaming, 'I'm gonna fuck you up! Watch your back in the parking lot!' All over a damn $11.99 workbook."

"I had a parent state that I bullied her child and that was why he had a 13% in the class. Never mind all of the assignments he never turned in. The meeting was with all of his teachers, and according to her the reason the student was failing was because our district had conspired, since the student was in kindergarten, to make his educational experience a living hell."

"I called a student's mother to discuss her poor attitude. The mother told me, 'Oh, well you must've provoked her.'"

"I wrote on a student's (who is struggling) progress report (kindergarten) '_____ is respectful and considerate. Please continue to work on letter sounds at home.' The progress report was returned with a ranting letter on the back. 'I work with my child for 5 hours a week on letters, maybe you need to teach the assignments better in class.'"

"A parent told me her daughter was behaving badly because she switched her cereal to whole wheat."

"Parents threatened to have an arrest warrant for forgery because there was no way their kid had forged a signature on a test grade. It had to be me because their kid didn't do such things."

"A parent threatened to 'beat my ass.'"

"A parent told me to my face that the reason I was divorced was because I didn't love my own child and since I had lost some weight I thought I was better than everybody else."

"I told a parent that his daughter was a good kid and he told me that's what he was thinking about while making her."

"After a student of mine was in a fist fight with another student, the boy's mother came in and screamed at me. She taught her child to fight back, so he shouldn't get in trouble for it at school. Then she told me, if I ever write him up again for hitting back, she will reward him with a video game because he is doing what she taught him to do."

"I had a mom who was pissed off that she would have to get up and get out of bed to bring her child to school because we reported her for truancy. I teach 5th grade and the child had failed twice already yet No Child Left Behind says she better pass that test and now my pay is tied to it."

"A parent screamed at me for not being able to cure her child's (imagined) disability. When I suggested she speak to our Special Ed. department she yelled, 'She ain't retarded!'"

"I had a student who liked to disappear into the restroom for extended periods of time. When this was brought up at a conference, the parent said that it was my fault because he felt so ostracized in my classroom that he would rather spend his time in the restroom. This is a second-grade class."

"I got berated by a parent for her student getting a B on a progress report. The principal called me in the middle of my class to let me know that I needed to inform parents when a student's grade drops dramatically. Uh, hello, the progress report is your warning."

"A student got written up and the parent had an issue with the assistant principal. On her way out of the building she yelled out, 'You ain't nothin' but a house nigga! You can lick my ass *and* my pussy!'"

"I was told by a parent that I had to earn their child's respect. A 5-year-old may not call me a bitch, nor may he walk around kicking people because he wants their toys!"

"I had a student tell me to fuck off in the middle of class because he was playing a game on his phone and I asked him to give it to me. His mom told me that I was probably just being racist."

"A kid picked up a chair and threw it across the room. The mom's response was, 'Well, he did have an egg for breakfast the other day.'"

"A parent accused me of making her son autistic."

"I told a mother I would no longer clean up after her 8-year-old son. I explained that I cannot stay after school for hours cleaning the classroom because I have papers to grade, lesson plans to write, and my own family to get home to. She wrote me the following letter, 'Leaving books out isn't a behavior problem. Being a teacher is about taking time to make your class a clean and safe place. Grading papers and writing lesson plans is part of being a teacher. I understand wanting to get home to family but you chose to be a teacher. Teaching is a job, yes, but telling me you value your life more than teaching my child isn't what you tell a parent. Teaching is a choice and a lifestyle, not just a paycheck.'"

REALLY REAL EMAILZ: PARENT EDITION

From: A. Looney

To: English Teacher

Subject: Blanche's English Project

Dear Ms. Morris,

I want to know what you said to my daughter about her project to make her so upset. She is upstairs in her room right now crying hysterically and saying that she is stupid over and over. She does not normally talk like that about herself so I am wondering what you said to make her feel this way. Did you say that she is stupid? She is working very hard on her project and if I found out that you were speaking negatively to her I would be very upset. Please email me back a.s.a.p. to let me know what has been going on in class to make Blanche so upset.

A. Looney

From: English Teacher

To: A. Looney

Subject: Re: Blanche's English Project

Dear Ms. Looney,

I have said nothing to Blanche to warrant such behavior. In fact, she has been coming to class late every day and has not been completing her work. I have been extremely respectful to her and often ask her if everything is okay and if she needs extra help. I have been nothing but encouraging to your daughter.

Best wishes,

Ms. Morris

From: Dick Schwett, Ph.D.

To: Erma's Teachers and Administrators

Subject: Learning Opportunity for Erma

Dear Teachers and Administrators,

During the last three weeks of school, my daughter Erma and I will travel to Hawaii to observe the transit of Venus. We will explore Hawaiian geology and Hawaiian culture including native sky lore and the celestial navigation of the Polynesians. Erma will also interview Native Hawaiian Elders. I am asking that you please excuse my daughter from all assignments during this time, including all final exams.

Thank you,

Dr. Schwett, Ph.D.

The following email from the Ass. Principal came soon after:

As you can see from her father's email, Erma has yet another amazing opportunity to learn from real world experiences by traveling with her father. Please freeze her grades and exempt her from all assignments, including her final exams.

Gunther was an interesting young fellow with the ability to write scholarly papers at home, and occasionally pass in-class multiple choice tests that were announced well in advance. Yet in class, he could barely read or write, failed most quizzes, and generally stared off into the distance while drooling profusely. I tried to contact his parents about the incongruity between his classwork and homework, but I never received a reply. Towards the end of the semester, all of Gunther's work was at kindergarten level, including his homework and papers. I sent an email to his mother, expressing my concern for the drop in his level of effort and failing grades. I received the following email in response:

From: Emma Royd

To: English Teacher

Subject: Concern about Student's Performance

Dear Ms. Morris,

Thank you for your email and your concern for my son. I am going to tell you the truth. Ever since Gunther was in preschool I knew something was wrong. He wasn't learning what the other kids picked up quickly. As the years went on, he had trouble learning to read and write. I have two younger children who are very bright and surpassed Gunther years ago. I have had him tested over and over again but his doctors maintain that there is nothing wrong with him, other than a low I.Q. To compensate, I have done most of my son's work for him. Besides writing his papers, I spend about four hours a night drilling him so that he can pass his tests. The reason his grades have slipped recently is because, quite frankly, I am tired. I am a lawyer, and I work very hard. I am also a single parent raising three kids on my own with no financial help of any kind. My ex-husband left us a few years ago for a 19 yr. old and moved to another country. He left no forwarding address and cannot be reached. I had a bad injury a few weeks ago and basically gave up on Gunther. I know I shouldn't be doing his work for him, but I don't know what else to do. He cannot do anything on his own. If you can offer any advice, I'd really appreciate it. Otherwise, he is probably going to continue to fail his classes because I can't be his tutor anymore.

Sincerely,

Emma Royd

I didn't really have any advice for Gunther's mom, other than utilizing the school's resources like academic support and hiring a private tutor. I tried to highlight Gunther's positive skills, like friendliness. After another week or so Gunther's grades started to improve and his papers were back to the previously high standard, so I knew his mom had resumed her position as his tutor.

From: Anita B. Slapt

To: English Teacher

Subject: My son's grade

Dear Ms. Morris,

Please help me understand this situation. My son does his homework for your class every night. He also studies and reads each night. He says he pays attention in your class. Yet still he fails your tests and has a D. If my son is doing all that he can, then obviously you can't teach. Please shed light on this matter.

Thank you,

Anita B. Slapt

From: Maya Kidsux

To: English teacher

Subject: Summer Reading

Hello. It is the night before school begins and I am extremely concerned for my son. He just noticed today that he had a summer reading assignment that is due on the first day of class. The assignment was to read a 350 page book in preparation for an in-class essay. Although my son did receive the paper in the mail which explains the summer reading assignment, he only read the front of the paper which described the history assignment. He completely missed the other side which outlined the literature assignment. My son is a hardworking student and should not be penalized on the first day for an honest mistake. I am asking that you make an exception and excuse him from the first assignment.

Thank you so much for your understanding,

Maya Kidsux

From: English Dept. Head

To: English Teacher

Subject: FWD: Problem with teacher

I received the following email today. See me when you get a chance so we can talk about how to handle this.

From: Mia Syko

To: English Dept. Head

Subject: Problem with teacher

Dear Dept. Head,

I would like to discuss a problem my daughter is having in her English class. Ms. Morris consistently calls on her even though she does not raise her hand. This puts a lot of undo stress and pressure on my daughter, who happens to be very shy. I hope you'll agree that education is meant to raise and not diminish a child's self-worth. Putting my daughter on the spot like that has been slowly eroding her self-esteem. Don't you think this type of teaching method goes against the ethics of public education? My daughter does not want to participate and she should be able to opt out if she chooses.

Please speak with Ms. Morris about this matter.

Ms. Syko

I gave my tenth-grade class a district-mandated research paper. It was made very clear that the students were supposed to compile and critically analyze research to present both sides of a controversial issue. One student I'll call "Herbert," handed in a paper that was made up of only his opinion about women, specifically about how they are inferior to men and should not be paid the same wage or given equal rights. I explained to the student that if he did not rewrite the paper he would receive a failing grade since there was no research used. He told me that it wasn't fair that he would fail the paper because of his personal views. I tried to clarify why he needed to rewrite the paper. It had absolutely no research. He argued with me that his research was based on his own observations. I said that did not count as valid research. He said I was unfair, refused to rewrite the paper and failed. Soon after I received the following email:

From: I.M.A. Moran

To: English teacher

Subject: Problem with Research Paper

Dear Ms. Morris,

I am writing on behalf of my nephew Herbert. He has informed me that you recently gave him a failing grade for a report he turned in. I have read the report and must say I disagree with the grade he received.

While you are teaching the students to be fair and balanced in their research, you were not fair and balanced in your grading of this paper. There are two sides to every issue and Herbert chose the side which he felt was not being represented in your class. The class reading materials did not contain the evidence that the other side has on this matter. So Herbert had no recourse other than to present his position as unsupported opinion.

While I do agree that the paper did not follow the prescribed directions, I strongly feel that it deserves to at least pass, based on the quality of the writing alone. Herbert feels very strongly about this issue, and you have made him feel that he can no longer express his opinions in class.

Please let me know how I can meet with you in person to discuss this matter further.

I emailed back and explained my reasoning once again. I also attached the grading rubric for the assignment, which clearly showed how heavily the paper relied on scholarly research. Thankfully, Herbert's uncle failed to contact me after that.

From: A. Nell Retentive

To: English teacher

Subject: Buford's grade

Tonight, my son and I were looking at his updated grade in English which is a D, 67.6%. I'm disappointed with the outcome in English given everyone's efforts to support Buford. After two personal meetings with you and many emails back and forth, as a collective we seem to have fallen short. At our last meeting, you said that reading quizzes are a particular problem for Buford. He scored poorly on a book check, as if he hadn't read the book yet he told us he had. On the most recent reading quiz Buford scored well, with a solid B. This is a noticeable improvement, I'm sure you'll agree.

Buford is at a loss as to why all the homework he turned in recently was marked so low, given that he says he put so much effort into it. He received a 5 out of 10, which is failing. As you know, he missed quite a few classes because he was sick. Did you mark these assignments down because he was absent? Have you updated all of the homework grades in the online grade book? The last homework was entered one week ago.

Are all the grades for the course entered at this point? Buford said there is a group work assignment that is not there, among other things. At this point, are there assignments that Buford can redo or is there any wiggle room to "X" out a low scoring grade at the teacher's discretion?

This school year has been very challenging for Buford. I'm hoping to get a better understanding of what went wrong and how his grade can go up before the end of the semester next week.

A. Nell Retentive

From: English teacher

To: A. Nell Retentive

Subject: Re: Buford's grade

Good morning. I understand your disappointment; however, final grades in my class are not complete yet as they are not due for another two weeks. I do still have to enter the project grade as well as the last essay the students wrote as part of their final assessment.

I do think Buford's absences compounded his already difficult time in class, and while one quiz showed an improvement, he failed the selected response portion of the final assessment. His homework assignments received half credit because he only answered half of the questions.

The final exam will weigh heavily on his final grade, so let's see how that goes, and I can touch base again before final grades are submitted.

Sincerely,

Ms. Morris

From: A. Nell Retentive

To: English teacher

Subject: Re: Re: Buford's grade

When I asked Buford about the questions he skipped on the homework, he said he didn't know he was supposed to do them. It's unfortunate that the distinct pattern of his missing certain questions on several assignments wasn't caught early. It seems the questions he missed played a large part in the discussions while he was absent and affected his final assessment.

In hindsight, Buford definitely would have benefitted from access to teacher notes or some kind of written guide to help fill in the time missed. In the future, I think Buford would benefit from someone looking over the homework to make sure he is on track. Answering the right question is one of his fundamental challenges. As I think I mentioned in the meeting, a middle school English teacher discovered this for us. It wasn't that his answers contained the wrong information, it was that he misunderstood the question or did not see it at all.

Usually final exams don't benefit Buford's grade because he gets nervous, but let's see what happens. Let's touch base before grades are entered.

Thank you,

A. Nell Retentive

From: English teacher

To: A. Nell Retentive

Subject: Re: Re: Re: Buford's grade

Good morning. After entering all of Buford's final grades including his final exam, it looks as if he will end with a D. Again, I appreciate all the effort Buford has put in this quarter--I know it has been difficult for him, and I wish him all the best next semester.

Sincerely,

Ms. Morris

To: English teacher

From: Al Sew-Rententive

Title: Grade of D

I think we all failed Buford. We know what he's capable of, we know what impediments he faces, we saw some improvement but, in the end, this will discourage, rather than encourage him. And that is very sad.

Al Sew-Rententive

From: A. Nell Retentive

To: English teacher

CC: Al Sew-Rententive

Title: Re: Grade of D

I just want to add that given the trajectory was an improvement, it's unfortunate that the outcome can't be different. Exams as a general trend are always lower than his semester grades. Last year, they pulled down his grades in two classes and ultimately affected the semester grades.

Does Buford's work really reflect a D student's effort? His world is very difficult. He is extremely intelligent and yet struggles with his own perception of being stupid. He is sensitive and his self-esteem suffers.

English has been his least successful class this year. In all other classes, teachers supported his extra efforts and the grades reflect that. Given that you must see Buford's improvement, is there really no way to have the semester grade reflect that?

From: A. Nell Retentive

To: English teacher

CC: Administrator

Title: Re: Re: Re: Re: Re: Buford's grade

Today I researched the District Grading Procedures for Grades 6-12. I had a question concerning teacher discretion. I refer to Item 27 under Procedures which states, "When a teacher has evidence that a student demonstrates a higher level of performance than a calculated marking period grade indicates, a teacher may record a higher grade in consultation with an administrator."

I would like to request that Buford's grade be updated to a C based on the effort he put forth. This has been a year of trial and error for Buford. We are all trying to put the pieces together for him to be successful. A hand up now would go a long way towards encouraging him. This would safeguard his fragile self-esteem.

Sincerely,

A. Nell Retentive

Several administrators suggested that I refrain from answering any further emails from Buford's parents. They continued to meet with administrators until they received the grade change that they wanted.

One week into the new school year I received the following email from the guidance counselor of one of my students:

From: Guidance Counselor for Orville

To: English Teacher

Subject: FWD: Requesting new English class

Dear Ms. Morris,

I am forwarding a message I received from the mother of Orville Fullah-Crapp. Can you give any insight into this matter?

Forwarded Message:

To: Guidance counselor

From: Mr. & Mrs. Fuller-Crapp

Subject: Requesting new English class

To whom it may concern,

We would like to request that our son be removed from Ms. Morris' Honors English class immediately and placed into the challenging academic environment in which he belongs. Orville feels that there are many struggling readers in his class, and there is simply no rigor in the assignments that he has been tasked with. Orville has tested at genius levels in math and science and deserves to be in an academic setting where his peers have equal abilities and potential. He has learned absolutely nothing new in his English class, and based on the assignments he has brought home, we are not surprised.

We are requesting that Orville be removed from his current English class and placed into one where he truly belongs. Also, for the time that he remains in Ms. Morris' class, we have excused him from the last two homework assignments because we feel they are simply "busy work" and have no academic merit.

Thank you for your understanding in this matter,

Mr. & Mrs. Fuller-Crapp

I explained to the counselor that we were only one week into the school year and that it would be ridiculous for them to judge the rigor of the class based on the assignments that were given. I also defended the assignments with the fact that I was following the district's curriculum and doing the same work as every other Honors English class. I offered to meet with the parents to explain this further, but they refused to meet with me. Instead, they met with the counselor and an administrator to discuss my incompetence. The administrator was adamant that Orville stay in my class and that the parents reserve judgment until the end of the school year. The parents petitioned the district and sent weekly emails of complaints to my administrators. Meanwhile, Orville was rude and often cruel to other students and did less than stellar in my class.

From: English Teacher

To: Jack Haas

Subject: Concern about student

I am writing to express my concern over Ferdinand. He has not shown up for most classes this quarter and is failing the class. If he does not meet with me to assess how he can make up the work he has missed, he will lose credit and have to take the class again.

Thank you.

From: Jack Haas

To: English teacher

Subject: Re: Concern about student

So what do you want me to do about it?

III. ADMINISTRATION

"Against stupidity even the Gods struggle in vain."

Friedrich Schiller

PROTOCOL

Wilbur slept a lot in class, but other than that he showed no unusual signs that would indicate drug use or psychological problems. He was quiet when awake, and did his work with some amount of effort. You could imagine why I thought he was joking when he interrupted me, in the middle of a class discussion, to tell me that he was overdosing on OxyContin. It went exactly like this:

8:45 A.M.

ME: Most people don't realize that what Hamlet is saying here is very literal…

Wilbur stands beside me and speaks softly.

WILBUR: Miss, I need you to call 911.

ME: Hold on a second… what?

WILBUR: I think I'm overdosing.

The color starts to drain from Wilbur's face.

ME: Overdosing? On *what?*

WILBUR: I took a bunch of OxyContin when I first got to class, but I think I took too many.

Wilbur proceeds to lie down on the floor in front of me. As I grab my cell phone and begin calling 911, the rest of the class starts to chat, casually, as though nothing out of the ordinary is taking place.

ME: Hi. I'm a teacher and I have a student in class right now who is on the floor and he says he overdosed on OxyContin. Okay, thank you.

I call security and they contact the nurse. Then I kneel on the floor beside Wilbur.

ME: Are you okay?

WILBUR: I think so. I don't know. I feel weird.

ME: Everything is going to be okay. There is an ambulance on its way. You're going to be alright.

The bell rings and 29 students step over Wilbur to exit the classroom. They do not pay him any attention. One student, who is usually a bit of a jerk, asks me if Wilbur is okay and if he can help. I thank him and ask if he could tell the teacher next door what is going on and ask him to come over. I speak gently to Wilbur to try to calm him and keep him conscious. I ask if he has been depressed and he nods yes. I ask if his parents know how he has been feeling and he says no. I inquire where he got the meds and he says from his dentist. The color in his face begins to return. Suddenly the school nurse enters with a wheelchair and starts yelling at Wilbur.

NURSE: What is going on? What did you take?

Wilbur stammers and starts to look pale again.

WILBUR: I took... Umm... Just a few pain killers.

NURSE: Why? Why did you take those? Were they prescribed to you?

WILBUR: Yes, my dentist gave them to me.

NURSE: For what?

WILBUR: I got my wisdom teeth out.

NURSE: When?

WILBUR: Last year.

NURSE: Sit up. Get me the bottle. I want to know exactly how many you took.

Wilbur rolls around in confusion a little. I offer to get the bottle. I ask Wilbur if it's in his bag

173

and he nods yes. I find the bottle in his backpack and hand it to the nurse. Before she can say anything else a crowd of people rush into the room. There are lots of EMTs with a stretcher, all of the assistant principals, the principal and a few others I don't recognize. No one addresses me. They put Wilbur on the stretcher and everyone follows him out, including the nurse. I am left alone, sitting on the floor of my classroom, wondering what the hell had just happened. Before I could pull myself off the floor, one of the assistant principals sticks her head into the room.

ASS. PRINCIPAL: Are you okay?

ME: I don't know. I mean, I think so.

ASS. PRINCIPAL: You didn't follow protocol.

ME: Huh?

ASS. PRINCIPAL: During a medical emergency a teacher must always press the emergency call button and alert the office, who then alerts the nurse. She is the one who determines if it is necessary to call an ambulance.

ME: Oh, I didn't realize. It's just-

ASS. PRINCIPAL: Next time press the call button.

The Ass. Principal exits. Just as I stand up, my next class comes racing into the classroom, with no knowledge of what had just happened. So I put on my game face and prepare to talk about Homer's Odyssey.

*NOTE: The general wait time for a response to the call button is 15-20 minutes if you are lucky enough to get an answer at all. Even if the office responds right away and tells the nurse immediately, by the time she makes it over from her office at least ten minutes will have passed. If she then makes the decision to contact an ambulance, there is that much more wait time.

I didn't hear about Wilbur for a few weeks and I didn't have his contact information. Eventually, he came back to school and handed me a note. It read, "I'm really sorry about what happened. I'm so embarrassed. Thanks for being so understanding, it really helped. Happy Halloween!"

174

Wilbur graduated and came back to visit the next year in an EMT uniform. He had decided to become an EMT to help people have a better experience in an emergency situation than he had. This was a beautiful full circle, as it never usually is.

A BIT OF AN INTROVERT

Bilbo's behavior was very strange during the first few weeks of the school year. On the first day, he wore a hooded sweatshirt and tied the hood around his face very tightly. When I asked him to remove his hood, he ignored me. During the next class, he had his hood tied just as tightly and kept his head down the entire class. I tried to engage him, but he completely ignored me. By the third class, he was sitting with his head between his legs. I asked him if he was okay and told him that he needed to sit up, but of course he never moved or showed any signs that he had heard me. I asked my supervisor for help and she said that I should be firm and tell him that if he didn't sit up and take off his hood he would need to leave. By class number four he was actually sitting on the floor underneath the desk with his hood tied so tightly it covered his eyes. I got down on the floor and asked if he was okay. He didn't answer. I told him that if he didn't get up off the floor he would need to leave the class. There was no response.

I reported back to my supervisor and she said she could handle this quite easily. She came to the following class where he was under the desk again. She stood in front of his desk and firmly told him to get up. He didn't stir. She tried again, but there was no response. She got down on his level and yelled at him to get up and when nothing changed she got up and told me to tell the Ass. Principal to handle it.

The Ass. Principal was sure that she could take care of this issue. According to her, I was a new teacher and didn't have much experience dealing with these types of students. She would show me how it should be done.

She marched into the class and did the same thing my supervisor did but got a little angrier and a little more animated. After yelling at Bilbo to get up for a while, she called me into the hallway and said, "Just ignore him. If he wants to sit under the desk, let him." So I spent the rest of the semester trying to communicate with a student who was tucked into a sweatshirt under a desk. I'd ask how he was, how his day was going and if he planned on doing any work. I'd even slip papers and pencils under him. I never got a response and after a while the class forgot he was even there.

THREE STRIKES AND YOU'RE STILL NOT OUT

Dictionary.com defines plagiarism as "an act or instance of using or closely imitating the language and thoughts of another author without authorization and the representation of that author's work as one's own, as by not crediting the original author." Essentially, it is cheating. Passing off someone else's work as your own is a major problem. Why would students write their own papers when they can easily copy one from the endless amount of websites they have access to? If integrity isn't enough to keep a student honest, then hopefully the fear of disciplinary consequences would prevent them from cheating. Right?

Well my school, along with many other high schools and universities, has adopted a very soft approach to dealing with the overwhelming amount of plagiarism. The most common excuse that students give for plagiarizing is that they did not realize they were doing it. Now I'll admit that it is an understandable mistake to quote something and not say where you got it from. But here I am talking about something very obvious, one that you wouldn't need a lesson to prevent. I am talking about taking huge chunks or in some cases the entire paper from someone else and passing it off as your own words.

Since students claim they have a lack of knowledge in this area, it has become something to blame the teachers for every year. We are expected to explain to the student what they did wrong, how to properly cite sources and make sure they understand how to avoid plagiarizing in the future (even though we probably already went over this ad nauseam in class). We are also expected to let them redo the assignment with no penalty. Whereas plagiarizing one's paper used to mean at least receiving a zero for the assignment, and sometimes even detention/suspension/expulsion for academic dishonesty, it is now an opportunity to redo the assignment for a better grade! There is no record of how many times a student plagiarizes so they can pull this trick as many times as they wish, always using the same excuse that they didn't know and getting away with it on the occasion that they are not caught.

Several English teachers proposed doing an extensive lesson on plagiarism and how to avoid it in class (which most do at the beginning of the year anyway) and giving each student a form to sign that acknowledges they know what plagiarism is and what the consequences would be if they were to plagiarize their work. The administration decided that even if students sign the form, they are likely to make the same mistakes, and we should show that we understand the plight of young writers.

Needless to say, a lot of kids plagiarize. And a lot of them are just downright lazy about it, cutting and pasting whole articles into their papers and not bothering to change the fonts to match each other.

That is what "Goober" did. He emailed me a research paper that was almost entirely comprised of a Wikipedia article. I found the article by googling merely one sentence. I discussed the consequences with him and allowed him to do the rewrite, since he claimed that he uploaded the wrong paper (the second most commonly used excuse). Since he claimed that he had the correct version on his computer I gave him the weekend to email it to me. The second paper that I received was also mostly plagiarized from an internet article. I discussed this with him and explained that he would be receiving a zero since he was now aware of his actions and how to prevent making the same mistake twice. He now claimed that his brother wrote the paper and that it wasn't his fault that his brother chose to plagiarize. "Clearly," I explained, "having your *brother* write the paper is *also* cheating so that excuse does not work."

I received an email a few days later from an administrator about Goober. Apparently he was very upset about his zero. The only reason he had his brother write the paper, he said, was because he was very sick, and I only gave him two days to rewrite it. I explained to the administrator that the reason I only gave him two days to rewrite it was because he claimed that he had already done it, and merely needed to email it to me. I never received a response after that. I angrily accepted Goober's third draft.

Guess what happened next? Parts of the third draft were plagiarized. I contacted the same administrator to ask that disciplinary action be taken. I received the following response:

"Spoke with student. Student understands the gravity of his actions but explained that he really does not understand what plagiarism is and was not merely trying to pass off the work as his own. Please re-teach the student how to properly cite sources and allow for rewrite."

By draft four I was ready to explode with frustration, but thankfully it never came, and Goober received a zero, which is what he should have gotten in the first place.

Other commonly used excuses for plagiarism:

• "It must be a coincidence." Sometimes high school students are able to write the exact same paper as a scholar on the internet, by accident. It's pretty much a modern day miracle.

• "I never said that I wrote it." Even though they put their name on it, they never announced within the paper itself that these were their own words. So obviously, they are not at fault.

• "I have a photographic memory, and I thought I was writing my own thoughts." Amazingly enough, some students take pictures of essays with their brains, and then later copy directly from those photographs, mistaking it for their own thoughts.

• "Someone else uploaded the paper for me and uploaded the wrong one!" Parents and siblings are giant morons when it comes to uploading the right file for their family members. For some reason, they constantly upload essays from the internet and put their family member's name on it!

- "But I didn't copy the whole thing! Some of those words are mine!" Yeah, and the words that are yours are the shitty ones.

- "Everyone does it." Yes, that is very true. But you are the fool who got caught. It's cool though, you can just rewrite that shit over and over until you get the grade you want!

REAL WORLD SCENARIOS

In my school, we have two grading policies that are a bit nonsensical. While one would think that in high school we should prepare students for "the real world" by showing them that they must actually earn their grades, the administration does not seem to agree. The first is a policy mandated for all students within the district. It states that if a student receives a grade that is higher than a zero but lower than a fifty percent, it automatically gets bumped up to a 50%. For example, if a student gets one question right on a ten question quiz, they automatically get four more free points added on to their final score for showing "minimal effort." So if a student basically farts on every assignment for an entire semester, they'll end up with 50% in the course. If they put just a dab of effort into a few assignments, they'll pass.

The other policy that is unwritten, but widely understood, is that a teacher should rarely, if ever, give a student a zero. To put a zero into the grade book, the teacher must have successfully contacted the parent or guardian of the student to inform them of the missing assignment and provide opportunities for reassessment. If no contact has been made, even if the student's home phone number is out of service etc., the teacher must give the student half credit for the assignment, *even if it does not exist.* To clarify, even if a student tells me to shove my assignment up my asshole, if I do not speak with his parent, he still gets half credit!

Let's examine real life situations where this might be the case:

Scenario: I pay absolutely none of my $150 credit card bill for the month and avoid their phone calls.

Outcome: $75 is *not* applied towards my outstanding balance. Instead, my credit score goes down and I owe more money in late fees.

Scenario: My house is on fire. I make absolutely no attempt to put the fire out.

Outcome: Not half, but my entire house burns to the ground.

Scenario: My pet is hungry. I give him absolutely no food.

Outcome: My pet starves. I get arrested for animal cruelty.

Several school districts across the nation have adopted a "no zero" grading policy. Basically, a teacher is no longer allowed to give a zero for work that has not been completed. The rationale behind this is that failing to complete assignments is a behavioral issue and grades should reflect a student's ability level and not their behavior. Instead of receiving a zero for a test or assignment that has not been completed, students are marked with a comment stating that the assignment is incomplete. The student's grade is then based on whatever work he or she has actually done, with no penalty for the missing work.

Some teachers have refused to use this policy, citing the fact that it teaches students to have no accountability and some have been suspended and/or fired over it.

Speaking of school policies that need revision, my district's discipline policy leaves much to be desired. There is a huge push in our nation's schools to lessen or even eliminate suspensions, expulsions and referrals to law enforcement. The U.S. Department of Education and the U.S. Department of Justice jointly released initiatives to "assist school districts in promoting positive learning environments and limit unnecessary disciplinary action." The idea is that when you suspend a student, they are missing valuable learning opportunities which is counterintuitive to their education and behavioral improvement. In an effort to reduce suspensions, interventions are supposed to address students' social and emotional requirements, identify future behavioral problems and teach students appropriate behavior.

The Behavioral Education Plan is designed to teach appropriate behavior to keep students in school rather than suspend them when they break rules. Instead of just removing students from the classroom and school, the plan outlines interventions that are aimed at keeping students in school to improve academic achievement and graduation rates. My school district, along with many others across the country, has adopted this plan. Under this plan, there is a range under which a student can receive consequences for their actions. Whenever possible, it is advised that the lowest level (or least severe) consequence be implemented. The result has been, at least from what I have seen, a student body who understands that they can get away with almost anything with little or no consequence.

For example, for making inappropriate gestures, verbal or written comments, including cursing, the most extreme consequence one can receive is "community service, peer mediation and temporary removal from class." An example of this would be just a few weeks ago when a student said, "Open the motherfucking door you bitch!" to me, and only received a chat with an administrator about appropriate language. The student refused to apologize.

For plagiarizing, meaning copying someone else's work; forgery of a parent or teacher's signature or cheating, a student may be asked to write an apology (though no one will check that they do), and the most that can occur is peer mediation, and community service (though I have never heard of a student doing community service for these violations.) I have rarely, if ever, heard of a student receiving *any* consequences for these behaviors.

For engaging in inappropriate behavior of a sexual nature (e.g. indecent exposure) a student may only receive peer mediation and a time out, and the highest consequence for this is a few days suspension. A sexual attack may receive as little as in-school suspension. Students are caught in the act on a regular basis, including two who were going at it on the main staircase as students entered the building at 7:30 in the morning. Those two got two days suspension.

For making a bomb threat or threatening a school shooting, a student may

184

receive as little as community service and peer mediation. For physically attacking an employee of the school system or other adult, including intentionally striking a staff member who is intervening in a fight or other disruptive activity, a student may receive as little as having to write an apology or a talk with a school counselor. These same consequences are suggested for setting or attempting to set a fire. For using or threatening to use a knife or other implement as a weapon with intent to cause serious bodily harm, a student might only receive a few days of in-school suspension. If a student possesses an incendiary or explosive device, material, or any combination of combustible or explosive substances that can cause harm, it is suggested that they write an apology and have a chat with their counselor.

If the consequences for such severe and harmful behavior is so negligible, you can imagine that there are no consequences for things like being consistently late to class or skipping. Under the current attendance policy, if a student misses more than four classes without an excuse note they will lose credit for the class and have to retake it. This policy might encourage students not to skip if it was adhered to. But students can obtain a contract that states they will try to come to class more often and teachers are obligated to sign it. If this contract is signed, the student gets credit at the end of the semester. If the contract is not signed, the administrator will most likely go into the system and pass the student anyway, especially if he or she is a senior.

They have made it so difficult for teachers to remove credit from a student that it is almost impossible. If a student has missed most of their classes it is very likely that they will not pass. However, teachers are required to provide enough makeup work for these students for them to pass. It is a common occurrence for a student to come to a teacher on the last day of the school year with an attendance contract, and they are expected to sign it, even if there are no more classes for the contract to be fulfilled. If a teacher makes a habit of not signing these contracts, he or she is seen as a nuisance to administration and accused of "not being a team player." In the end, there is much less aggravation if you just sign the contract and let the kid pass, regardless of the fact that they rarely showed up and did almost nothing in your class.

HIS FUCKING PHONE IS OF UTMOST IMPORTANCE

I had a student whose name closely resembles that of a type of dinosaur. To protect his identity I'll call him "Raptor."

Raptor slept through most of my classes, no matter what tactics I used to keep him awake. He would sprawl out across two chairs in the back row and prop his feet up on a desk. I actually preferred him asleep because when he was wide awake, he would ask every member of the class for lotion until he got some, take his shoes and socks off, put his feet up on the desk, and lather up his legs and feet. It was quite disgusting.

One day, after I finally got the class settled and ready to take a test, Raptor stood up and yelled, "This class is not fucking starting yet!" I looked at him in shock. "Excuse me?" I answered. "That's right," he said calmly. "This class isn't fucking starting until I get my fucking phone."

"Raptor, you can't use that language. You're going to have to leave."

"*No.* I'm not going anywhere until I get my fucking phone!" he replied.

Raptor came to the front of the room, pulled a stool in front of me, sat on it with his arms crossed and said, "Now who took my fucking phone?" I stepped out from behind him. "Excuse me. You can't just take over the class like that."

"Yes, I can. And I'm not moving until I get my fucking phone. Someone took my fucking phone and I want it *right now.*" I explained to Raptor that perhaps if he had approached me about his problem without cursing I would be willing to help him. But at this point I didn't care that someone took his phone. I was more concerned with his disrespectful behavior.

Without moving he said, "Yeah, what're you gonna do? You gonna fight me?" I started to walk past him to call security to remove him. He saw me move and began to pat his chest and throw his arms in my face.

"You wanna go? You wanna fight me?" he yelled. I just laughed at him and told him I was calling security. It took them about 25 minutes to get to the classroom. We spent every minute of that time in silence because every time I tried to speak, Raptor interrupted me and reminded the class that he wanted his fucking phone. (By the way, in the midst of this I offered to *call* his fucking phone, but he said that it was disconnected.)

When security finally got there, I pulled them into the hallway and explained the situation. They *seemed* to understand what I was saying. They entered the room and ordered the students to stand up and proceeded to pat them all down. They also emptied all of their backpacks and questioned them heavily. During this, I explained that the issue was not Raptor's missing phone (which they did not find), but rather his cursing at me, threatening me and preventing the class from starting. They ignored me and said they would handle that later. They took Raptor to the security office to record the details of his missing phone. I sent an email to the Ass. Principal and this is the response I received:

"Had discussion with Raptor about his disrespectful actions. Student seems to understand the seriousness of what he did. Please call parents for follow-up."

The phone number listed for his parents was disconnected. He informed me the next day that he had forgotten that he left his phone in his locker, and it was not actually stolen. I asked if he was sorry for the way he treated me. He shrugged and said, "I dunno," then walked away.

FLIPPING A BRICK

Bertha was a very friendly young lady. She always took the time to ask how my day was going and how my weekend was. In fact, a few weeks into the semester, she started to ask me if I needed money. I thought she was joking, so I always said, "Yes, of course. I'm a teacher. We *always* need money." She would then tell me that she would hook me up. I thought this was all very cute and playful until Bertha pulled out a huge wad of cash during class.

In the middle of a class discussion, she asked if I had change for a hundred dollar bill. "No Bertha," I said, "I don't carry that kind of cash. And I doubt that you do either." She immediately flashed an enormous mass of bills, with a hundred wrapped around the top. My mouth dropped and the eyes of every student in the room lit up. "Okay, put that away. I don't want to see it." She put the money away and said, "I don't understand why teachers get so pressed about money." I told her to be quiet. She replied, "Ms. Morris if you need money so bad you could just flip a brick." I did not know what this meant, but I assumed it wasn't good. "That's okay, Bertha. I don't need your help." She pulled out a twenty, got up and slid it across my desk. "Here. I feel bad for you." I pushed it back to her and told her not to feel bad for me. I said that her behavior was inappropriate. She shrugged her shoulders and sat down.

I looked up "flip a brick" online and found out that it meant selling drugs, but it wasn't specific about what kind. I guess I should have realized that drugs come in the form of bricks, or packages shaped like bricks. It turns out that I was not as hip as I had once thought.

I referred Bertha to security and the assistant principal and reported that she had told me that she sells drugs and should be searched. No one answered me and I forgot about it, until the next class.

Bertha was now conducting shady transactions in the back row of my classroom. I couldn't see what she was giving out, but I could see that others were giving her money in exchange for something. I called her into the hallway and told her that I didn't like what she was doing in my class. She didn't deny it. She tried to recruit me again. "Ms. Morris, you could make so much money and you wouldn't have to be so pressed all the time."

"Bertha, I want you to stop this," I said. "You are never to ask me that again, and you are never to sell anything in my class. I don't care if it's chewing gum." She shrugged her shoulders and said, "Okay."

During the next class, Bertha asked to go to the bathroom. It didn't occur to me at the moment that she would probably sell drugs when she got there. She left the class, went into the hallway, and right in front of the open classroom door she conducted a little transaction. I ran into the hallway and screamed at her to get back into the classroom. She did but told me to "chill" on her way back in. "I will not chill! Were you just selling drugs, Bertha?"

"Yeah," she replied.

"So you're admitting it!" I said.

"Yeah," she answered.

"And you admit that you have drugs on you right now?"

"Yeah, it's just a little weed. Nothing serious."

"I'm sorry Bertha, but I'm going to have to call security."

"That's cool. Mr. Boots (the head of security) is my man. He'll be cool about it."

I pressed the security button, but no one came. Class ended and Bertha left. I officially wrote her up for selling drugs in my class. A few days later the Ass.

Principal called me down to her office to discuss the situation. After I explained the situation, she agreed that it sounded very serious, and she would notify the principal and school police officer immediately. A few days after that, I got an email from the Ass. Principal explaining that the principal felt the evidence I gave did not warrant Bertha being searched by the school's police officer. He said that I should leave the matter alone.

What does a kid have to do to be searched? Perhaps sprinkle drugs on top of my head? I thought. Bertha announcing that she had drugs, and my actually witnessing a transaction in my class was not enough, so I dropped it. Soon after, the class was working on research papers about controversial issues in the U.S. It was hard to get Bertha to focus and work on anything. She kept asking me if she could write her paper about legalizing marijuana. I said it would be okay, as long as she took the project seriously and did actual research.

To my surprise, Bertha turned in a beautifully written, scholarly research paper about medical marijuana dispensaries in the U.S. Her paper began with the following line, "As the stubborn economic downturn has forced the state of California to take painful steps to balance its budget in recent years, it has increasingly turned to one of its newer industries to raise much-needed revenues: medical marijuana dispensaries." I was blown away by this sentence; not because it was so well written, but because Bertha could barely read or write at an elementary school level. I looked up the first sentence of her report and found that her entire paper was merely a New York Times article. I asked her if she wrote her paper by herself. She asked why I wanted to know. I responded that I was amazed by how well written it was. She thanked me and took the credit. Next, I told her that it was easy to figure out that she completely copied her article from the internet. She said "oh" and admitted to it right away, with little to no shame. I emailed the Ass. Principal the following email:

From: English Teacher

To: Ass. Principal

Subject: Office Action (Urgent)

Bertha completely copied a very important research paper from the internet. We have been working on this paper for several weeks, and her entire paper was merely a New York Times article with her name on it. She did not show much remorse for this when I spoke with her. I would like for there to be a consequence so that she understands the seriousness of what she is doing. I have tried to contact her parents, but none of the numbers listed are in service.

In response, the Ass. Principal asked to meet with Bertha and me in person to discuss this matter. We met in her office and here is how the meeting transpired:

ASS. PRINCIPAL: Bertha, we are here to discuss a paper that you wrote.

Me: No, she didn't write any of it. She completely copied it, word for word, from a newspaper article.

ASS. PRINCIPAL: Is that true?

BERTHA: I mean, I don't know.

ASS. PRINCIPAL: What do you mean?

BERTHA: I wrote *some* of it.

ME: No she didn't. It is, word for word, a *New York Times* article.

ASS. PRINCIPAL: May I see the paper?

ME: Sure.

ASS. PRINCIPAL: Why did you write about marijuana?

BERTHA: I dunno.

ME: The assignment in the curriculum is to research a controversial pro/con issue.

ASS. PRINCIPAL: And you let her write about drugs?

ME: Well, it is a very controversial issue right now, and the curriculum doesn't specifically state what issues they are allowed to write about.

ASS. PRINCIPAL: But you should know, Ms. Morris, that this is inappropriate.

ME: I felt that maybe if the student was allowed to write about something she took a personal interest in, she might focus and do her work for once. And given my history with Bertha, I know that she has an extreme interest in the legalization of marijuana.

ASS. PRINCIPAL: But that is not appropriate. Students should not be writing about drugs. You should know that. Bertha, why did you copy your paper?

BERTHA: I dunno.

ASS. PRINCIPAL: Don't copy work anymore. Write another paper about a different topic, okay?

BERTHA: Okay.

ASS. PRINCIPAL: Great. You can go now.

BERTHA: Okay bye.

ME: Is she not going to get any punishment for completely plagiarizing her paper?

ASS. PRINCIPAL: She knows not to do it again. But I don't think you should have let her write about drugs.

ME: It was supposed to be research based, and not include their opinions.

ASS. PRINCIPAL: Ms. Morris, you're a new teacher, and I suppose you don't know this, but writing about marijuana is not appropriate.

ME: Okay.

ASS. PRINCIPAL: Okay, thanks.

CAUSE FOR CONCERN

As mentioned in previous chapters, on the first day of school I have students introduce each other. Sometimes I ask them to choose three words to describe themselves. You can tell a lot by the words a student chooses. Some give very factual labels, such as brother, student, teen. Others stick to their hobbies and say runner, basketballer, footballer. Some students take the humorous approach and say something like "future favorite student" or "flat out pimp," while others use this opportunity to show me that they are not interested in participating in my activities such as, "I don't know" or "dumb, stupid, lazy." When Michael and his partner stood up I expected a standard answer. I was wrong.

Michael's partner introduced him as "Michaela" and she looked quite reluctant as she repeated his three words, "caring, quiet, tranny." I was about to correct her and say that it said Michael on my attendance list, but the word tranny cleared that up.

Besides that first introduction, Michaela stayed completely quiet in class for the next two months. She worked diligently and was an excellent student. Then suddenly she was absent for three straight weeks. Worried, I called home to ask about her absences. I introduced myself and before I could get the word "Michaela" out, the student's mom said, rather abruptly, "Thank you for your concern. My son has not been feeling well. Please send work to the main office for us to pick up," and hung up.

I dropped off work to the office every day, but it was never picked up. Another week went by and I was still concerned. I emailed an administrator. I was told that Michael would be coming back to school shortly and that I should excuse him from any of the work that he had missed during his absence. This is not the usual policy for absences. Students are generally held accountable for any work they may have missed. But I didn't want to rock the boat.

Michaela returned to school soon after that and when I asked her how she was feeling, she answered "What do you mean?" with a rather blank stare.

"I just want to make sure that you're feeling okay," I replied. "We've missed you."

"I'm not sick," she said, with a flat affect.

"Okay. I'm glad to hear that. Welcome back."

Now I was really confused. Ironically, in class that day we were having a discussion about gender roles in Shakespeare's *Macbeth*. Not long into the discussion Michaela asked to be excused. I asked if everything was okay and she walked past me and out the door without answering. Her friend Apple that she had been sitting next to asked if she could check on her. I agreed.

The friend came back at the end of class and explained that Michaela was having a hard time. I asked for more details and she said that she couldn't give me any. She had been sworn into secrecy.

Now I was really concerned. I went to speak with Michaela's guidance counselor in person. I told her everything that I knew and asked her to fill the holes for me. She said that Michael and his parents had requested complete privacy and that she could not tell me anything. I told her not to call him Michael because he prefers to go by Michaela. She was a bit surprised and said she had never heard that before.

Since I couldn't get any information out of the guidance counselor, I tried to forget about it until Michaela was gone for two weeks again. I spoke to another guidance counselor, who has a pretty big mouth, and she told me the details.

"You didn't hear this from me. That kid is suicidal and homicidal."

"Wait. What? What do you mean *homicidal?*"

"He has tried to kill himself numerous times due to gender identity issues. His parents refuse to acknowledge the fact that he identifies as a girl."

"That is horrible. Absolutely horrible. But did you say something about *homicide?*"

"Yes. He took pictures of himself in a dress and sent them to his friends. Then he freaked out and threatened to kill those friends if they showed the pictures to anyone."

"Well, I'm sure it was just a figure of speech."

"He brought a knife to school."

"*What?*"

"Yup. And his best friend Apple showed the cops a bunch of text messages that she received from him where he threatened to kill her."

"*Apple?* She's in my class! They sit next to each other for god's sake! Why wouldn't they tell me?"

"The parents don't want anyone to know anything."

"So has he been in jail this whole time?"

"No. He's been in an institution."

"And they didn't think that I needed to know about this? I'm his teacher. We talk about very sensitive topics in class like suicide and gender roles."

"I know but if the parents request privacy, the school has to follow."

"But I need to ensure the safety of the other students, especially Apple!"

She shrugged and said she understood. When Michaela came back to school a few days later, she was no longer sitting next to her friend. Michaela was out of school for most of the semester. When she was in class, I was always a little worried and went over in my head what I would do if she took out a weapon. I don't know what ever came of that situation but the following year I saw Michaela in the hallway in a floral dress. She had the same cropped haircut, mustache, and muddy sneakers yet she was proudly wearing the type of dress that little girls wear to church on Sunday. I called out to her and asked how she was doing. She smiled brightly, which I had never seen before and replied, "Great!" She seemed to be embracing her gender identity and it was nice to see.

NOT A TEAM PLAYER

For a while, the school had a very strict I.D. policy. Every student was given a picture I.D. and they were expected to wear it around their necks at all times. This became a huge disciplinary issue because, of course, students never wanted to wear it. It took a considerable amount of class time every day to check that each student was wearing their I.D., and to go through the line of questioning for all the students who were not wearing it. Those who didn't have one had to leave class to get a replacement sticker from the office. In classes where it was impossible to get kids to follow reasonable rules, the I.D. thing was a gigantic pain in the ass. But I went through the I.D. routine every day, just in case an administrator walked by.

One day, in a particularly unruly class, the Ass. Principal dropped in for a surprise observation. I had already taken twenty minutes to go through the dreadful I.D. check, and miraculously, every kid was wearing their stupid I.D. Yet the bigger miracle was that on a Friday afternoon, in a class filled with thirty struggling teens with major disciplinary and attention issues, the entire class was quiet and working diligently. Anyone who knew the typical context of the class would have been amazed at what I had gotten these students to do. It was no small feat and I was very proud. But apparently, that's not what the administrator was concerned with. I received the following write-up in my mailbox:

"I am extremely concerned that one student is not wearing his I.D. This is a very strict policy the school has been enforcing for various safety reasons, and Ms. Morris shows that she is not a team player by not enforcing the rules in her classroom. A copy of this form will be in her permanent file."

I was not given a chance to explain that the student's I.D. came off when he removed his sweatshirt. There was also no mention of the lesson plan or quality of student work. Apparently, just like students, teachers have a "permanent file" that follows them throughout their career. And my little transgression would remain there throughout my years, even though the I.D. policy was completely eliminated the following year.

WHAT IS THIS CCRAP?

A 2016 Educational Policy Primer

The issues of Common Core State Standards (curriculum standards for the nation), and the PARCC test that is administered to test for those standards, are extremely complicated. It is a matter of how far down the rabbit hole one wishes to go. I will introduce you to the essential facts, in case you are unaware of what this all means, and then I will share my personal experience with it as an educator.

I.   What is this CCRAP you speak of?

The Common Core State Standards Initiative is an "educational assembly" in the U.S. that specifies what K-12 students should know in English and math at the end of each grade level. According to their website, "The initiative seeks to establish consistent educational standards across the states as well as ensure that students graduating from high school are prepared to enter credit-bearing courses at two- or four-year college programs or to enter the workforce."[17]

The Common Core Standards are now the law in 46 states. The reason that most states have adopted the Common Core is not because they agree with it, but because they wish to receive competitive grants that were introduced on July 24, 2009, as an incentive for educational improvement.[18] To qualify, states had to adopt standards and tests that are supposedly "internationally benchmarked" to prepare students for future success. States could use their own standards and still qualify for the grants, but they were given extra points in their grant submissions if they agreed to implement the Common Core standards by August 2, 2010.[19] We are talking about $4.35 billion in federal funds. Some states, like Massachusetts, got rid of their own effective standards and replaced them with the Common Core, to get millions in federal funds.[20]

II. Cash Rules Everything Around Me

There is nothing wrong with having high standards for education, and most teachers already meet most of these standards in the classroom. But when taking a closer look at the origins of the standards there are several red flags. According to Diane Ravitch, former U.S. Assistant Secretary of Education, "There is absolutely no evidence whatsoever that these standards will improve achievement, enrich education, and actually help to prepare young people -- not for the jobs of the future, which are unknown and unknowable -- but for the challenges of citizenship and life. The biggest fallacy of the Common Core standards is that they have been sold to the nation without any evidence that they will accomplish what their boosters claim."[21]

According to the creators of the Common Core, they relied heavily on public feedback throughout the writing of the standards and assessments. But if you look at the section of "public feedback" on the Core Standards website it is quite deceptive. "First of all, calling the feedback 'public' is wrong: the organizers of the standards would not make public the nearly 10,000 comments they say they received from citizens. The summary quotes 24 respondents–less than 1/4 of 1 percent of the total–selectively chosen to back up their interpretation of the results."[22]

When researching the Common Core State Standards, I began to wonder who exactly created them. It is not an easy task to find the authors of the Common Core. But after much digging, I found a list of 135 people who created and revised the Common Core Standards. In all, only seven of the 135 members were actual classroom teachers and no one was a K-3 classroom teacher or had any training in early childhood education.[23] We are told that teachers helped create the standards, but that is simply not the case. Educators with actual classroom experience would be able to write standards and exams that are challenging yet developmentally appropriate. However, my concern is not really with the standards, but more with the test that was created to check that the standards are being implemented.

The PARCC (Partnership for Assessment of Readiness for College and Careers) test is a Common Core-aligned test designed by the for-profit company Pearson, which was paid $360 million in federal funds to write these exams.[24] Pearson is a multinational corporation, and the world's largest education company and book publisher, earning more than $9 billion annually.[25] They own nine publishing houses, including Penguin, Harcourt, Puffin and Prentice Hall. They also own part of the University of Phoenix.

Currently, Pearson produces expensive testing materials for 18 states in the U.S. Their contract in Texas alone is worth $500 million. They own the General Education Development tests (GED), the edTPA, and the NES, required teacher licensure tests that people pay over $100 to take. They also own the Quotient, a test for ADHD in students; the test for National Board Certification of teachers; the SAT-10, a test that measures reading and writing skills for grades K-2; and SuccessMaker, a digital learning curriculum that teachers have been forced to use in grades K-8. Pearson owns online for-profit charter schools called Connections Academy too. Obviously if a student uses Pearson texts and curriculum they will perform higher on Pearson's standardized tests. It's no wonder that Pearson was a major supporter of the creation of the Common Core Standards.[26]

Another way that Pearson rakes in the cash is by including product placements in their tests. In a 2013 English assessment, a reading selection included "root beer which was referred to at one point as Mug™ Root Beer. It was followed by a footnote, which informed test-takers that Mug™ was a registered trademark of PepsiCo."[27] They have also included references to IBM™, Lego®, FIFA® and Mindstorms™.[28] While Pearson will say they do not receive any money for these product placements, in many cases they are linked to the businesses which are mentioned. For example, Pearson recently partnered with Lego to create a line of educational products.[29] Also, IBM was awarded a contract in 2012 to create the "technology architecture" for the PARCC.[30]

Another alarming aspect of a private company owning these tests is that they have access to student data with very little oversight. Pearson may sell personal data related to individual children who have taken the PARCC. They cannot guarantee the security of this private student data, and have never made clear precisely how they will use it.[31] Not surprisingly, IBM has shown interest in storing this data.

So far there is absolutely no proof that the Common Core standards, Common Core curriculum, and Common Core testing, will in any way end what is referred to as the achievement gap.[32] This gap refers to the difference in achievement (including test scores, graduation rates, and college enrollment) between lower income and higher income students. This gap is present in all nations around the world.

The only nationwide study on the probable costs of applying the Common Core and PARCC estimates costs of almost $16 billion over seven years.[33] Currently, hundreds of millions of tax dollars are going to corporations for the creation of curriculum and tests as well as the technology used to implement the test, all under the guise of closing the achievement gap. But this ignores so many of the significant issues that are the cause of the achievement gap, such as poverty. The amount of homeless children in Colorado alone, a state which has adopted the PARCC test, has more than tripled in the last decade. Imagine what that money could do for those children. It could even simply provide them with a nourishing breakfast every morning. Obviously if a student is well-fed, they will perform better in school. "We know quite clearly that children who have quality nutrition, healthcare, as well as access to books via libraries with certified librarians, and all the other resources provided to children in particular zip codes, actually, have done quite well on standardized tests in the past. Yet, we continue to ignore this fact, and we continue to feed our children living in poverty only tests."[34] In order to pay for the creation of these assessments and the technology and materials they require, we disregard critical resources such as new books, smaller class sizes, librarians, nurses, counselors and much more.

In my own district, I have seen this huge waste of money firsthand. Millions have been spent on Chromebooks for the mere purpose of taking the PARCC test, a test that 15 states have recently dropped. Meanwhile, we are told that there is a budget crisis and, once again, teachers are warned of frozen salaries and higher rates for health insurance. Due to budget cuts, there are already much larger class sizes and fewer guidance counselors, social workers, teachers' assistants, librarians, psychologists, social workers, special education teachers, reading specialists, and security guards. Our massive school, with thousands of students, recently lost our sole police liaison due to funding issues. This is a huge loss for the safety and security of the students and teachers. We often have violent fights, gang activity, etc. that need police intervention, and the lack of that one police officer has led to quite an increase in these incidents.

Another aspect of our school that suffers due to budget cuts is funding for the arts, physical education, foreign language programs, and other subjects that are essential for the well-being and well-rounded education that our students deserve. As more money is provided for standardized tests, less money is available for the vital programs and services that all schools should provide.

III.   15-year-old Professors of Classical Roman Literature

Besides the sheer waste of tax dollars, there's the problem of the impossibility of the tests themselves. New York has given Common Core tests for the last two years, and both resulted in approximately a 70 percent failure rate state-wide.[35] The Nathan Hale Senate–a body, made up of teachers, administrators, parents, and students–voted unanimously that the PARCC test was inappropriate for the age groups it tests. "The vote was taken after careful consideration and much discussion and inquiry, including two school community forums.[36] It is basically public knowledge that students will perform poorly on this test. Yet according to the No Child Left Behind Act and other school reform processes, standardized test scores like these are used to fire teachers, reduce their pay, hold students back and close down schools.

Just to give you a general idea of how impossible the tests are, here is a breakdown of the reading levels required to understand the passages on the test. The Lexile number for proficient readers in 4th grade is around 800. Yet the passages on the PARCC are at a level of 1100, which is the average level of an 8th grader.[37] The average 11th grader reads at a 1250 Lexile range. Yet the reading selections on the PARCC go all the way to a Lexile level of 1470. To give you a more worldly application, reading a driver's manual requires a 1220, for a nurse to perform his or her job it's 1310, and for a scientist the level is 1450.[38]

Allow me to give you an even clearer picture of how the PARCC reading selections and essay prompts are inappropriate. Third graders are asked to write an essay on how a character's words and actions are important to the plot of the story. Fourth graders must analyze the structural elements of a Maya Angelou poem. Sixth graders write an essay that identifies a similar theme in two complex texts and compare and contrast the approaches each text uses to develop that theme. Seventh graders read and analyze a passage from *The Count of Monte Cristo* written in 1844; the ninth grade test includes an excerpt from *Bleak House*, a Dickens novel that is usually taught in college; and tenth graders are asked how Ovid structures lines in his poem "Metamorphosis" to add meaning to the events of the poem. If you are reading this, you are probably as smart as the average 10th grader. See if you can answer this question about this excerpt from a 2,000-year-old epic poem:

"But while he labored a pert partridge near, observed him from the covert of an oak, and whistled his unnatural delight. Know you the cause? 'Twas then a single bird, the first one of its kind. 'Twas never seen before the sister of Daedalus had brought him Perdix, her dear son, to be his pupil. And as the years went by the gifted youth began to rival his instructor's art. He took the jagged backbone of a fish, and with it as a model made a saw, with sharp teeth fashioned from a strip of iron. And he was first to make two arms of iron, smooth hinged upon the center, so that one would make a pivot while the other, turned, described a circle. Wherefore Daedalus enraged and envious, sought to slay the youth and cast him headlong from Minerva's fane,-- then spread the rumor of an accident. But Pallas, goddess of ingenious men, saving the pupil changed him to a bird, and in the middle of the air he flew on feathered wings; and so his active mind-- and vigor of his genius were absorbed into his wings and feet; although the name of Perdix was retained. The Partridge hides in shaded places by the leafy trees its nested eggs among the bush's twigs; nor does it seek to rise in lofty flight, for it is mindful of its former fall."

How does the poet structure these lines to add meaning to the events of the poem?

a)   He includes a flashback of the story of Perdix to show that Daedalus wanted to kill Perdix, and now Perdix enjoys a kind of revenge by seeing Daedalus mourning the death of his son.

b)   He includes a flashback of the story of Perdix to show that Perdix now lives in the shade but Icarus died trying to reach the sun.

c)   He includes a prediction that foretells that Daedalus will soon have to bury Perdix as well as his own son.

d)   He includes a prediction that foretells that Perdix will be fated to live an obscure life when he should have been a famous inventor.

I have several advanced degrees in English and I'm only 85% sure the answer is A. So, how'd *you* do? Now try writing a literary analysis about the poem. Go on. Do it.

Part IV. Damn Those Teachers and Their '93 Nissan Sentras!

According to a report issued by Pearson entitled, "Preparing for a Renaissance in Assessment" our current standardized tests aren't good enough though Pearson actually wrote many of them. The report notes that "without a systematic, data-driven approach to instruction, teaching remains an imprecise and somewhat idiosyncratic process that is too dependent on the personal intuition and competence of individual teachers."[39] How do they plan on fixing the problem of imprecise and incompetent teachers? Replacing them with computers! The PARCC uses computer algorithms to robo-grade student essays. The report states as a fact that the PARCC consortium will use automated essay scoring.

Speaking of the general putdown of teachers, Pearson's chief education advisors and authors of the PARCC Peter Hill and Sir Michael Barber (two men who have never taught in an actual classroom for even one day) also argue that the discipline of teaching must progress into a more closely controlled profession which will make it much harder to become a teacher and much easier to fire one too. This would require eliminating the practice of "teaching as a largely under-qualified and trained, heavily unionized, bureaucratically controlled 'semi-profession' lacking a framework and a common language."[40] After Pearson gets finished with the totally hopeless teaching world, it will be magically transformed "into a true profession with a distinctive knowledge base, framework for teaching, and well-defined common terms for describing and analyzing teaching at a level of specificity and strict control."[41] Seriously, when have you ever heard a career that requires a Master's Degree, several certificates which must be constantly renewed and a vast amount of training referred to as a "semi-profession?" Are there bad teachers? Of course! Just like any other profession, there are teachers who are burnt out, ineffective and/or just horrible people. But no other profession has those few failures color the public's general feelings towards all of them. Pearson's answer to the problem of teachers in general is to basically have all educational decisions made by their software and their system. Teachers will just be needed as a sort of supervisor or babysitter.

IV. Beating the Dead Horse to a Bloody Pulp

Whether or not you believe in standardized testing, you have to agree that our students are extremely overtested. Merely to take the PARCC exams, grades 3-8 will spend 10 hours testing. For high schoolers, it will take more than 11 hours. On top of that, high schoolers have to take a quarterly district exam, a midterm, a final, and several AP tests. Also, 10th graders take the PSAT and 11th and 12th graders take the SAT. The more ambitious students also take several SAT subject tests. Basically, the average high school student will spend between 20 and 30 school hours taking standardized tests. That is a lot of valuable instruction time that is wasted. Plus, it is just too much stress for a kid! According to education researcher Gregory J. Cizek, there is much research "illustrating how testing produces gripping anxiety in even the brightest students and makes young children vomit or cry, or both."[42] In fact, vomiting during the test is so common that some tests come with instructions for the examiner on what to do with a test booklet if a student barfs on it.[43]

In my classroom, the PARCC has made most students feel stressed out and inadequate. Even the highest achieving students find the tests exhausting and irrelevant. But for the struggling readers and writers in my classes, the consequences of these tests are much more serious. Many of my students read and write at a level that is many grades below where they should be. Several of my 10th graders read at a 3rd or 4th-grade reading level, for various reasons. The test is absolutely impossible for them. Most don't even try, which is a typical response to being made to feel dumb. The ones that do try are extremely anxious and confused. They have a million questions though I cannot answer any of them. This test is sending them the message that college is not an option for them, which is not true. The experience is the same for many special education students. They get almost none of their testing accommodations during the test and it severely impacts their performance. As I said, the tests must be administered on Chromebooks, which have to be carefully unplugged and specifically assigned, and then carefully plugged back in and locked down. This takes an absurd amount of time, time that we do not have.

V.   Break Stuff

Now that you know what a load of dung the Common Core tests are, you can go outside and throw things. Or you could join one of the many anti-testing movements that are rapidly growing. You have the right to opt your children out of any and all state standardized tests. United Opt Out and FairTest.org have guides for all fifty states. What happens to a child in a public school classroom is up to the parent. Do not let administrators scare you into taking tests. They may say that if you opt out the school will lose funding, it will harm the performance evaluation of your child's teacher and your child will be kept back or punished. Most of these are empty threats, and legally they cannot do any of this.

Many teachers have tried to support the opt-out movement by informing parents and students of their right to opt out and some have even refused to administer the test. Many face disciplinary action and possible termination. The power truly lies in the hands of the people on this one. Know your rights. Fuck those tests and fuck Pearson.

WORDS OF WISDOM

Several times a year, teachers are formally observed by administrators. They check to see that the teachers are following the curriculum, the school's standards, controlling the classroom, etc. Specifically, on the observation form that the administrators use, it asks for comments on the following: mastery objective, agenda, evidence of rigor, key messages, relationships, active teaching strategies, differentiation, closure, engagement, routines, literary strategies and equitable practices.

Here are some of the more interesting comments I've received from classroom observations made by administrators:

- Why is there only one light on?
- This is a wonky room with too much sunlight and a folding wall and too much extra space
- One of your curtains came down
- Students drinking lemonade, Coke, Gatorade etc.
- Open the blinds to let light in
- Some of your blinds are not raised at the same level as the others
- I can't hear the student in the back who speaks low

- One student is wearing a hat

- One boy is drinking juice

- Seats are too close together

- Don't sit with your legs like that (criss-crossed behind a desk)

- Students are squirrelly

- Calls students "guys"

- When you write on the board, it isn't in a completely straight line

After one of my observations by the Ass. Principal, she asked me to meet with her to discuss how it went. She opened with the following comment, "I've been thinking about the issues you've been having with classroom discipline. You're too nice. I've been doing this a long time and the best advice I can give you is to treat every student like a sack of shit, and then they will respect you." At this point, I wasn't going to argue with her. She had many, many years in the field. In the past when I tried to disagree with her she would put her hand up in a "stop" kind of way and say, "You're a young teacher." That was my cue to shut my ass up.

Later that day she found me in class and asked if she could have a word with me. In the hallway she whispered, "Remember what I said before about treating students like sacks of shit? Please don't tell anyone I said that." Can you all keep a secret?

FROM THE FRONTLINES

Part 3

I asked a group of elementary, middle and high school teachers to describe their most challenging or hilarious interactions with an administrator. Here is what I received:

"The principal called me in to discuss the fact that parents had complained that I did not understand my subject enough to teach it. He cited a teaching group I am in as evidence which supports this. The group is state mandated for all teachers."

"Last week I sat on a hornet and was stung below the waist. I had a terrible allergic reaction and I was crying. They refused to let me go home."

"I was told to fail 1st graders who needed resources, then lie to parents about it so they would come back the next year."

"I worked at a charter school that was under investigation for money laundering. The principal said, 'I'm about to retire so I'm not worried about them closing the school!' to the entire staff."

"After my first evaluation, the assistant principal said to me, 'I'm trying to think of something nice to say, but I just can't think of anything. Are you sure you want to be a teacher?' When I put in my resignation later that year she asked me what I was planning to do. I told her I still wanted to teach and she told me that I

210

shouldn't."

"I asked the assistant principal for ideas to help kids who couldn't read. She told me to put them on a miracle computer program which was 'better than a human teacher.' Guess which kids made no growth?"

"When I resigned my principal told me that my parents would be disappointed in me."

"When I asked the principal at my former school why male teachers got paid more than female teachers, and taught fewer classes, he told me 'that's just the way it is and there's nothing you can do about it.'"

"I had a male student choke me and they only suspended him for one day. They told me that I could not press charges because I had not filled out the proper paperwork. He was let back in the building the next day and I had the union call the administration. The admins told the union that they had detained him, which was a complete lie. He was roaming the halls freely."

"The fact that when we send kids to the administrator's office for discipline there is never any punishment. The kids walk out laughing and don't take anyone seriously."

"After demonstrating a lesson where students were engaged and obviously making progress, the principal's only comment was, 'Three students had their uniform shirts untucked.'"

"My mother-in-law passed away and when I got back from the funeral I received an email from my principal that next time I would need to schedule my substitute ahead of time. So I guess I'll just let my family know that they will have to schedule their deaths in advance."

"During my second year of teaching a tough female student pushed and threatened me. When she wasn't suspended, I asked why. The principal's response was, 'That would have put her over on her days. You want her to graduate, don't you?'"

"The principal got mad that students were talking during a tornado drill and said into the loudspeaker, 'If you talk during a real tornado you will DIE!'"

"I shushed my class twice during an observation and I was told that that is an ineffective form of behavior management."

"Principal wrote that I 'make good treats' on my official evaluation."

"Principal observed me teaching a lesson on words that end in -ig and rhyme. She told me that I should have taken the opportunity to talk about weaves, because my students might not know what wigs are and I need to be culturally sensitive. These are 5-year-olds and weave does not rhyme with wig."

REALLY REAL EMAILZ: ADMINISTRATIVE EDITION

From: English Teacher

To: Every administrator in the building

Subject: Office Action (Urgent)

As a warm-up to introduce the class to each other on the first day of school, I asked the students to discuss what they would do with a million dollars. "Wally" called out that he would drive a bus into the school. The room became quiet. I asked him to clarify what he meant. He said that he has always wanted to drive a bus into the school and if he had a million dollars, he would buy a big bus and drive it into the front of the school. I told him that it isn't funny to joke about such serious things, and he insisted that he was not joking.

Follow-up: Three months later an administrator emailed me back and said, "Wally will be forced to attend academic support for a number of sessions."

From: Guidance Counselor

To: Phil's Former English Teachers

Subject: Recommendation Question

Phil Phart would like to take Honors English next year but was recommended for regular. Last year his grades in English were D, D, F. This year his grades were F, D, D. He scored low on his verbal PSAT and very low on his writing skills. I would appreciate any insights into the recommendation that he continue in regular English. I would also like to help him understand what skills he should work on to improve his grades in English.

From: Phil's former English teacher (not me)

To: Guidance Counselor and Phil's English Teachers

Subject: Re: Recommendation Question

Phil's scores are not much higher than the lowest possible scores on the PSAT. He barely passed English. What evidence is there that he will do well in Honors? Just because a student wants a challenge does not mean they can handle it. Should students not need to qualify to be in a higher level class? Shouldn't they be able to maintain at least a B in the lower class before being switched into the higher class? If not, then if Phil wants to be in the social club that Honors classes have become, let him. After all, where's the rigor anymore?

From: Guidance Counselor

To: Phil's Former English Teachers

Subject: Re: Re: Recommendation Question

Thank you. I will relay this information to Phil.

From: English Teacher

To: School Counselor

Subject: Concern about Student's Well-Being

Hi. I am writing to express my concern about Ruth's wellbeing. Today, she fell asleep at her desk, and I saw several cockroaches crawl out of her hair and down her neck into her shirt. This did not wake her up. I did not want to embarrass her, so I did not say anything. What can we do to check that her living conditions are suitable?

From: School Counselor

To: English Teacher

Subject: Re: Concern about Student's Well-Being

Hi Ms. Morris. Thanks for letting me know. I'll contact social services, but that usually leads nowhere. There is nothing more we can do.

From: Harry's Mom

To: English Teacher

CC: Harry's Dad

Subject: Concern about Student Breakfast

Dear Ms. Morris,

My husband and I are writing you concerning our son Harry and his inability to eat breakfast in your class. We have a very hectic morning, and there is simply no time for Harry to eat breakfast. Even if there was adequate time for him to eat, he is usually nauseous in the morning. We send Harry to school every day with breakfast hoping that he will eat it in class when he gets hungry. Yet he recently informed us that you have forbidden him from eating in your class, and that this is a non-negotiable rule. Please allow our son to eat breakfast in class from now on.

Sincerely,

Mr. & Mrs. Pitts

From: English Teacher

To: Mr. & Mrs. Pitts

CC: Ass. Principal

Subject: Re: Concern about Student Breakfast

Hello Mr. & Mrs. Pitts,

I am sorry that Harry is not able to eat breakfast in the morning. I agree that this is an important start to a student's day. Unfortunately, it is a school mandated rule that students do not eat or drink anything (besides water) outside of the cafeteria due to various issues such as cockroaches and mice. Perhaps you can find a little extra time in the morning for Harry to eat?

216

Thanks,

Ms. Morris

From: Mrs. Pitts

To: English Teacher

CC: Mr. Pitts, Ass. Principal

Subject: Re: Re: Concern about Student Breakfast

Dear Ms. Morris,

Our son has informed us that you often have a cup of coffee on your desk during class. Why can't our son have a drink and his breakfast at his desk? You aren't any more important than he is, and he needs a nourishing breakfast to get through the day like anyone else.

Sincerely,

Mrs. Pitts

From: Ass. Principal

To: English Teacher

CC: Murray's Dad, Murray's Mom

Subject: Re: Re: Re: Concern about Student Breakfast

Dear Ms. Morris,

As per his parents' request, please allow Harry to eat breakfast in class from now on.

ECHOES DOWN THE CORRIDOR

Why do I continue to teach if it causes such misery? That is actually a very easy question to answer: I'm slightly insane. All joking aside, when you think of the best, most inspirational teachers you have ever had weren't they all just a little bit nuts? We're all a little insane, and we have to be to undergo the daily onslaught of stressful bullshit and keep showing up for more. (The "normal" ones must be part of the 50% who quit in the first five years.) But honestly, to me, there's something addictive about the daily challenges, outrageous as they are. I would never want a predictable, normal job, even if it paid a lot more. I'd be bored.

Sometimes teaching is impossibly hard and heartbreaking and infuriating and sometimes (though much less often) it's amazing, fun, and inspiring. But it is never boring or ordinary or reasonable. And it is always hilarious. And it is always important. When I look back on my career and life, I'll be happy to know that I dedicated myself to this daily adventure/battle/crusade… perhaps the most important one there is. (I must admit that I am currently writing this in July, and it's easy to be positive and sentimental during the summer. I haven't seen a teenager in about three weeks.)

Somehow, in the end, the great and inspiring moments (though few and far between) outweigh the absurdity. Teaching is an incredible profession that can potentially give one's life meaning. But if you're going to be a teacher, you should know what you're getting yourself in to. As you've read, it's crazy out there, and the craziness never ends, but your ability to cope with it gets much better. You have to get just as crazy in return. Most importantly, you have to learn to laugh, or you might actually strangle someone, or develop a terrible stress-related disease, like many of my colleagues.

You also can't expect much praise or recognition. Like my argument against students being mature enough to "rate" the performance of their teachers, students are often too immature to recognize effective teaching while it's in progress. According to author Darren Shan, "Students never appreciate their teachers while they are learning. It is only later, when they know more of the world, that they understand how indebted they are to those who instructed them. Good teachers expect no praise or love from the young. They wait for it, and in time, it comes." It wasn't until I began teaching that I fully appreciated the efforts of many of my college professors. I have also learned how critical it is to share the importance of what you have gained with those who have taught you. In recent years I have written many letters of gratitude to teachers I hadn't spoken to in decades.

In the summer after my first year teaching, I received a letter of gratitude from an almost freakishly mature student. This kid was so mentally and emotionally developed that it almost felt like I had one ultra-perceptive and brilliant adult in the class, amongst the other teens. Whatever I said, she was right there with me. She got it. If you're a teacher, you know the type. This is the rare kind of kid that seems to know more about life than even we do. To receive a letter from this student was beyond meaningful, especially because the letter came after she graduated when I could no longer do anything for her.

In the letter, the student said that she felt privileged to be in my class, she recognized how much energy I put into my lessons, and she will forever remember my non-judgmental and open atmosphere. A letter like this really does make a lot of the aggravation melt away. This one student was developed enough to express herself in an adult manner, and her words mean more than any insult or put down I have ever endured. Also, while not as articulate, many students are often able to express the effectiveness of the class if given the chance to do so.

219

At the end of the year, I give my students the opportunity to assess the class, and my teaching, anonymously. I explain to my students that most teachers do not feel that students are mature enough to evaluate the class and that responses that students give, unfortunately, reinforce that idea. I also tell them that this is something that is done in institutions of higher learning, and that I truly value their opinions as my students and I want to know how I can improve. While there are always one or two responses that tell me to go fuck myself or say that the class simply "sucks," it is amazing how many students are able to communicate their feelings about the class in a helpful way.

One student expressed that many classes made him feel like a robot but that my class allowed him to think "deeply and insightfully." Another student said that my positive attitude made her more eager to study English, which means a lot because it is hard to remain positive amongst such rampant negativity. Others have called my class "off the beaten path," "engaging," "interesting," "mind-opening," "refreshing," "challenging," "creative," "thought provoking," "beneficial," and a class that made them want to learn. One student shared that he really came to appreciate me as a teacher. He even added, "That may sound superficial, but I say it with complete sincerity." Another said that he "appreciated [my] efforts to make English an enjoyable experience."

A student who was particularly quiet and withdrawn wrote, "It's been a while since I have gotten to have a teacher who is energetic and fun, someone who made me want to learn. In the last couple of years, I've had horrible and boring teachers, teachers that I despise, and I guess I lost sight of how much I enjoyed actual learning," which shows that you never really know who you're impacting. A student also reported that my class "made me wonder a lot about what I believe in, which is really good." I agree. I aim to have students question their beliefs and assumptions and the fact that one of them realized this is remarkable.

While these are only a few students out of hundreds who were able to express themselves in a positive way, it is unbelievably significant. I try not to lose sight of the fact that you cannot always tell when you are making an impact.

Each year when I prepare to teach *Night* by Elie Wiesel I have a hard time with the amount of responsibility a Holocaust text seems to carry. I want the text to affect them, make them think deeply and question our world. I want it to build compassion and a sense of duty to improve society. I don't, however, want to give them nightmares, scare them or make them loathe the human race. I often wonder if it is worth the amount of emotional energy it takes to teach this material.

The feelings of apprehension become stronger when I first introduce the text and several students get angry. They question why they have to read about the Holocaust *again*. They are sick of it being, "shoved down their throats." They want to read something cheerful, lighthearted and maybe even funny. They want to read something they might enjoy.

One student, in particular, was furious. I listened to his concerns and I genuinely shared mine. At the end of the semester, he stood up and asked to read a statement to the class. I cringed when I heard the first few lines, but was genuinely shocked as he continued.

"When teachers talk about the Holocaust, what are they trying to get us to understand? Obviously it was terrible, there is no denying that. But how is instilling graphic and gory images into the minds of young children progressing the world? How does reading about how life and joy were permanently drained out of prisoners make me a better person? It wasn't until recently that I discovered that remembering the Holocaust isn't about scaring you or making you feel terrible or mortified by the images and stories you are forced to learn about. It is about questioning your ideals about humanity. The Holocaust makes you look at the world in a new light. It makes you question evil and the capacity of evil. It makes you ask yourself what the boundary is between your well-being and someone else's devastation. The Holocaust puts you in the darkest places of your mind when you imagine the horrors that have been shared with you. It makes you question the strength of your faith, your will and your beliefs. The Holocaust is important to teach and to learn because it makes you ask the tough questions and explore the darkest corners of your mind."

This is exactly what I wanted them to get, and not only did this student get it, he was able to express it on paper as well. You can't always expect this type of reaction. You have to keep a little nugget of faith inside, cheesy as that may sound, and hope that you aren't wasting your time, energy, youth and ultimately, your life.

It is also the idea that whatever you feel like discussing, whatever feels important to you (within reason) you can present to your class. You have your own built-in audience who has no choice but to sit in your little world for a few hours each week and experience the atmosphere of you. I love that this group of teens has to look at the quotes that I feel are inspiring, and hopefully read books that I have chosen and ponder ideas of my choosing. It is a very powerful feeling and, although the negativity is often too dominant, the endless possibilities of the classroom keep calling me back each day, each year. I'm not done yet.

ABOUT THE AUTHOR

Jane Morris is the pen name of a teacher who would really like to tell you more about herself, but she is afraid she'll lose her job. She has taught English for over 10 years in a major American city. She received her B.A. in English and Secondary Education from a well-known university. She earned her M.A. in writing from an even fancier (more expensive) university. She loves dogs and trees and other things that can't talk. She has a loving family and cares about making people laugh more than anything else. Follow *Teacher Misery* on Instagram, twitter, and tumblr and visit TeacherMisery.com to learn about ways that teachers can vent their misery without fear of reprisal.

Appendix A. Artifacts from Students in their Natural Habitat

This appendix provides examples of the array of inappropriate and uncivilized material that teachers encounter on a regular basis. These documents serve as a record of the cultural beliefs and behaviors of adolescents in the early 21st century.

1. Middle school break-up letter

I can't be wit you no more. This other girl I know wants me to go with her. You don't know her she go to Aldine Middle. She in 7th grade like I should be but she 14 so she should be in 8th grade. She got that ass and those tet tetis and my birthday is March 29 and she told me if I go wit her I can Fuck her on my birthday. Plus she a crip so I will be wit her.

2. Students often include inappropriate drawings on papers they turn in to the teacher.

26. Briefly explain

3. I intercepted this "Bae Application" in my eleventh grade class.

1. Name, Age, Phone number
2. Body Count? (If over 5 please dispose of this)
3. How long are you going to wait to take me on a date?
4. Do you know anyone that can whoop my ass? Ex sister, Ex, Baby mother, cat
5. Can you fight? If so, you will fight all the thirst niggas on my social media accounts
6. Dick length? Stroke game 1-10?
7. Shoe size
8. Go inside your boxers pull out your dick, compare it to a fruit
9. Can you drive? (If not please recycle this)
10. How long before you eat me out?
11. If a police car A leaves the station @ noon going 35 mph. If police car B leaves the station @ 12:10 going 45 mph. Do you think you can make me squirt before both police cars arrive?

4. A fifth grade teacher asked her students to comment on the idea of karma.

Karma would hurt me because I fart in my dad's coffee when he's not looking.

5. This question was asked in a middle school health class. Other questions included, "If you poke a hole in a condom, will it protect against STDs and diseases?" and "Do three heads come out the vagina?"

    Would a plastic bag work as a condom?

6. Students have no filter, and do not know how to hold back awkward questions and comments about a teacher's personal life.

    Ms. Do you like watching TV or what? Are you lonely? I can live with you.

7. A first grade teacher asked her students to write the lyrics to their favorite song.

huntin loo...in for
a dolla this is
fucking awesome
walk inta the clab
like what up I got a
big cock I'm so
pumped I bought
some shit from a
thrift shop ice and th
The people are so damn frost

8. This anonymous letter was left on a teacher's desk.

9. This was the title of a formal essay I received in my eleventh grade class.

10. A high school teacher asked his students to list their goals for the New Year.

In 2012 I want to stop
Somking.

Smok more weed.

Do my best in School.

11. This illustration shows how children can be brutally honest.

Citations

1 Marsh, Sarah. "Should Schools Do More to Protect Teachers from
    Cyberbulling?" The Guardian. n.p., 24 May 2014. Web.

2 "A Silent National Crisis: Violence Against Teachers." www.apa.org. n.p., n.d. Web.

3 Kravets, David. "Student Who Created Facebook Group Critical of Teacher Sues
    High School Over Suspension." Wired.com. Conde Nast Digital, Dec. 2008. Web.

4 Ward, Paula. Punished for parody, student sues school. Pittsburgh Post-Gazette.
    January 2006.

5 J.S. v Bethlehem Area School District, Commonwealth Court of Pennsylvania, 18
    February 2002.

6 'At the End of the Year, I'm Setting Her on Fire': How Pupils Posted Death Threats
    on Rate My Teacher Website." Mail Online. Associated Newspapers, Nov. 2010.

7 Goss, Patrick. "French Courts Say 'non' to 'Rate My Teacher'" TechRadar. N.p., 8
    Mar. 2008. Web.

8 *Ibid.*

9 Moreno, Feliz. Ratemyprofessors.com: Take the reviews with a grain of salt. The
    Santa Clara, May 2011.

10 Koenig, Rebecca. "What You Need to Know About Yik Yak, an App Causing
Trouble on Campuses." *The Chronicle of Higher Education.* 26 Sept. 2014.

11 *Ibid.*

11 Morris, John-John. Hovering Parents Bully Teachers. The Baltimore Sun, March,
    2008.

12 https://www.commonapp.org

14 Ludden, Jennifer. Helicopter Parents Hover in the Workplace. NPR. February, 2012.

15 NIH Publication No. 11-4929, 2011.

16 *Ibid.*

17 "Frequently Asked Questions." Common Core State Standards Initiative. Retrieved
    March 13, 2015.

18 "President Obama, U.S. Secretary of Education Duncan Announce National
    Competition to Advance School Reform." U.S. Department of Education. July
    2009.

19 Fletcher, G. H. "Race to the Top: No District Left Behind." T. H. E. Journal, 2010.

20 Ravitch, Diane. "The Biggest Fallacy of the Common Core Standards." The
    Huffington Post. TheHuffingtonPost.com, n.d. Web. 13 Mar. 2015.

21 *Ibid.*

22 "Comments Pouring in on Common Standards, But You Won't See Them."
    Education Week. n.p., n.d. Web. 13 Mar. 2015.

23 http://www.corestandards.org/assets/CCSSI_K-12_dev-team.pdf.

24 "What the New Common Core Tests Are — and Aren't." Washington Post. The
    Washington Post, n.d. Web. 13 Mar. 2015.

25 Figueroa, Alyssa. "8 Things You Should Know About Corporations Like Pearson

That Make Huge Profits from Standardized Tests." *www.alternet.org*. Aug. 2013.

26 Anderson, Nick. "Common Set of School Standards to Be Proposed". The
  Washington Post: A1. 10 March 2010.

27 Strauss, Valerie. "Eighth Grader: What Bothered Me Most about New Common
  Core Test." Washington Post. The Washington Post, 8 May 2013. Web.

28 *Ibid.*

29 http://labs.pearson.com/perc_55316/

30 http://www.pacificmetrics.com/press_release/pacific-metrics-and-ibm-to-develop-
technology-architecture-for-the-partnership-for-assessment-of-readiness-for-college-
and-careers/

31 "Common Core Talking Points - UNITED OPT OUT: The Movement to End
  Corporate Education Reform." UNITED OPT OUT The Movement to End
  Corporate Education Reform. n.p., n.d. Web. 13 Mar. 2015.

32 Carnoy & Rothstein, "International Tests Show Achievement Gaps in All
  Countries", Economic Policy Institute. 15 January 2013.

33 McGroarty, Emmett, and Jane Robbins. "Controlling Education From the Top: Why
  Common Core Is Bad for America." Pioneer Institute and American Principles
  Project (2012).

34 Cody, Anthony. "Children Need Food, Health Care, and Books. Not New Standards
  and Tests." Education Week (2010). Web.

35 Ravitch, Diane. "The Biggest Fallacy of the Common Core Standards." The
  Huffington Post. TheHuffingtonPost.com, n.d. Web. 13 Mar. 2015.

36 Hagopian, Jesse. "New Seattle Test Boycott Erupts: Nathan Hale High School Votes
  to Refuse to Administer a Common Core Test." I AM AN EDUCATOR. N.p., 25
  Feb. 2015. Web.

37 Walsh, Russ. "PARCC Tests and Readability: A Close Look. Rider University, 2015.

38 *Ibid.*

39 Hill, Peter, and Michael Barber. "Preparing for a Renaissance in
  Assessment." Research.pearson.com. Dec. 2014. Web.

40 *Ibid.*

41 *Ibid.*

42 Gregory J. Cizek, "Unintended Consequences of High Stakes Testing - P-12,"
  Educational Measurement: Issues and Practice, Sep. 2001.

43 Susan Ohanian, "Collateral Vomitage." www.susanohanian.org. 14 Mar. 2002.

Made in the USA
San Bernardino, CA
19 February 2019